A GUIDE FOR GUARDIANS AD LITEM

IN

PUBLIC LAW PROCEEDINGS UNDER THE CHILDREN ACT 1989

A GUIDE FOR GUARDIANS AD LITEM

IN

PUBLIC LAW PROCEEDINGS UNDER THE CHILDREN ACT 1989

BY

STEPHEN PIZZEY AND JEFF DAVIS

London: TSO

Authors

Stephen Pizzey
(MA CQSW Dip Soc Admin)
Guardian ad Litem and Head of Social Work Department,
Great Ormond Street Hospital for Children NHS Trust

Jeff Davis
(MSc BA LLB CQSW Dip Soc Admin)
Guardian ad Litem

Legal Advisers

Peer Le Fleming
Solicitor, Gardner and Croft, Canterbury
Member of Children Panel

Jan Stanton
Solicitor, Stantons, Strood
Member of Children Panel

Published for Department of Health under licence from the
Controller of Her Majesty's Stationery Office.

ISBN 011 321879 6

FOREWORD

I am delighted to write this foreword because I feel sure that this reference book will be seen as a "must" for all those involved in Child Care Law. Stephen Pizzey and Jeff Davis are highly skilled and experienced guardians ad litem; there can be few others in this field who are as well equipped to write upon this topic.

Since the implementation of the Children Act 1989 the law and its associated professionals have focused on the child and his or her welfare when a family finds itself in crisis. Consequently, the guardian ad litem, in particular specified proceedings, has moved centre stage. Furthermore, as a result of this Act the demands made upon a guardian ad litem have become even more complex through the advent of additional parties and experts. It must always be remembered that in child care proceedings it is the guardian ad litem who speaks solely for the child. Other parties frequently view the issues and facts from a subjective standpoint and so, even though a hearing about a child should be inquisitorial, an adversarial approach tends at times to manifest itself, not least because decisions are being taken as to whether a child should be moved away from the parental home.

Because of the guardian ad litem's objectivity and independence great reliance is placed by the courts upon the guardian ad litem's report. There is a continuing need for guardians ad litem to be clear about how they should carry out the vital case preparation work and the writing of the report. In my view, this book is an invaluable addition to the material available for the guardian ad litem who wishes to ensure not only that every aspect of a case has been appropriately explored and reported, but also that such is properly and fully presented to the court. The authors cover each part of the guardian ad litem's responsibilities in this difficult, and at times, highly stressful field with a clarity, conciseness and thoroughness which should be an object lesson to any of those who seek to write an instructive book of this nature.

Our children of today are tomorrow's seed corn. In today's world it is more important than ever that they should be protected and assisted throughout their early and adolescent years. If the procedures and tenets advocated in this book are followed, then indisputably in the years ahead a major step towards helping and supporting them will have been taken.

The Hon Mr Justice Cazalet

ACKNOWLEDGEMENTS

We are extremely grateful to the Members of the Reference Group who read and annotated a copy of the draft text and generally contributed to our understanding of the subject area. They provided us with considerable support and encouragement.

Peer Le Fleming and Jan Stanton generously gave their time over the course of several meetings during the preparation of the guide. We are grateful for their steadfast support, advice and constructive criticism.

David Cook and Derek Gardiner kindly proof read the guide and assisted with the editing.

We have appreciated the involvement and encouragement of The Hon. Mr Justice Cazalet, both as a member of the Reference Group and for agreeing to write the Foreword.

The South Yorkshire Panel of Guardians ad Litem and Reporting Officers provided a draft copy of the report format developed by their local Family Courts Business Committee, some of which has been incorporated into the report format suggested in Part II of this guide.

The authors of Children Law and Practice, David Hershman and Andrew McFarlane, kindly gave permission for the "Grounds for a Care or Supervision Order: Check-Chart" to be reproduced in Part IV of this guide.

Judith Timms, author of the "Manual of Practice Guidance for Guardians ad Litem and Reporting Officers" helped us ensure that there was a consistency of approach between both guides.

The guide has undergone extensive revision during the course of its production and we are indebted to Jennifer Burgess and Eileen Farrier for typing the initial drafts and especially to Marlene Wallace for undertaking the word-processing of successive revised drafts and the integration of comments from the Reference Group.

The guide was commissioned by the Department of Health. Throughout the project the Department were in close consultation and provided detailed comments on legal, policy and practice issues. Particular thanks are due to Arran Poyser of the Social Services Inspectorate, and Margaret Vallance and Sue Ball of Community Services Division.

Stephen Pizzey and Jeff Davis
February 1995

PREFACE

A guardian ad litem is the person who represents the interests of children in specified proceedings under the Children Act 1989.

This guide covers the role of the guardian ad litem in those specified proceedings. Its purpose is to provide a reference book for guardians ad litem with a description of, and advice about:

- the appointment of the guardian ad litem;
- the powers and duties of the guardian ad litem;
- the courts' requirements of the guardian ad litem;
- the investigation and report of the guardian ad litem for each application;
- the role of the different professionals involved in the proceedings and the relationship between the guardian ad litem and those professionals;
- magistrates' and judges' expectations of guardians ad litem;
- the court structure and procedure;
- each application under the Children Act 1989 for which they may be appointed.

Throughout the guide the child is referred to as male and the guardian ad litem as female (although in the Act the guardian ad litem is referred to as male). 'Guardian ad litem' means a guardian ad litem appointed from a Panel of Guardians ad Litem and Reporting Officers. The law and case law used in this guide are understood to reflect the position as at November 1994.

CONTENTS

PART 2 – THE GUARDIAN AD LITEM'S INVESTIGATION AND REPORT

PART 3 – THE GUARDIAN AD LITEM AND THE COURT PROCESS

Appendices

List of Figures

LIST OF ABBREVIATIONS

All ER	All England Law Reports
CA 1989	Children Act 1989
CYPA 1969	Children and Young Persons Act 1969
Fam Law	Family Law
FCR	Family Court Reporter
FLR	Family Law Reports
FPC (CA 1989) R 1991	Family Proceedings Court (Children Act 1989) Rules 1991 (SI 1991/3095)
FPR 1991	Family Proceedings Rules 1991 (SI 1991/1247)
GALRO	Guardian ad Litem and Reporting Officer
SI	Statutory Instrument
WLR	The Weekly Law Reports

PART 1

FUNCTION OF THE GUARDIAN AD LITEM

CHAPTER 1
INTRODUCTION

Independent social work representation by the guardian ad litem in care proceedings was introduced in 1984. Nine years previously, the Children Act 1975 had introduced provisions for the appointment of guardians ad litem following a recommendation from the Report of a Committee of Inquiry into the Care and Supervision provided in relation to Maria Colwell[1]. She died after returning home, when an application by her parents for the discharge of a care order which was not opposed by the local authority was granted by the court.

In 1984 local authorities were required to establish panels of guardians ad litem and reporting officers when, in addition to the guardian ad litem's appointment in adoption proceedings, it became possible to appoint guardians ad litem in care proceedings in the juvenile court and access proceedings[2].

The Children Act 1989 extended the role of the guardian ad litem and increased its importance. The guardian ad litem is appointed in *specified* proceedings which are so called to identify the types of proceedings in which a guardian ad litem may be appointed. Guardians ad litem are required to advise the courts on allocation, timetabling and on how to keep delays to a minimum in the interests of the child's welfare. Under court rules they have specific duties for case management.

The guardian ad litem is the independent person who is appointed by the court to represent and safeguard the interests of children in public law cases. Sir Stephen Brown, President of the Family Division[3], has stated:

> "It is vital that the independence of the guardian in carrying out his or her duties on behalf of the child in any proceedings should be clearly recognised and understood. Since it is the responsibility of each local authority to establish a Panel of Guardians in its area . . . it is vitally important that the position of the guardian should not be compromised by any restriction placed directly or indirectly upon him or her in the carrying out of his or her duties."

The guardian ad litem is also an independent adviser to the court and to the child. Her powers and duties are set out in the Children Act 1989 and the two sets of Rules:

---

1   Report of a Committee of Inquiry into the Care and Supervision provided in relation to Maria Colwell (1974) London: HMSO.
2   Guardians ad Litem and Reporting Officers (Panels) Regulations 1983, (SI 1983/1908).
3   R v Cornwall County Council ex parte G [1992] 1 FLR 270.

- The Family Proceedings Rules 1991, part IV; and
- The Family Proceedings Courts (Children Act 1989) Rules 1991.

The former set of rules apply to the High Court and county court and are referenced in the footnotes of this guide. The latter set of rules apply to the family proceedings (magistrates') court and are used in the main text. Any significant differences between the two sets of rules concerning the role of the guardian ad litem have been highlighted in the guide.

In specified proceedings, also known as 'public law cases', the guardian ad litem must be either:

- a member of a panel of guardians ad litem and reporting officers, or
- the Official Solicitor.

The provision of panels of guardians ad litem and reporting officers continues to be a local authority responsibility[4]. There are 54 such panels covering England and eight covering Wales which are run either by single local authorities or by consortia of local authorities. The operation of a few of the panels has been contracted out by the responsible local authority to voluntary child care organisations.

Guardians ad litem[5] are drawn from the following groups:

- self-employed social workers;
- employees of a local authority;
- employees of a voluntary organisation; and
- probation officers.

Unless the court is satisfied that it is not necessary to safeguard the child's interests, the court will appoint a guardian ad litem in all public law cases affecting a child. The guardian ad litem will normally be appointed at the commencement of the proceedings and her role lasts for the duration of the proceedings. Even in circumstances where a child or young person is found to understand the nature of the proceedings and is believed to be competent to give instructions to a solicitor, the court still requires the independent view of the guardian ad litem[6].

The guardian ad litem must safeguard the interests of the child, taking account of the child's wishes and feelings, having regard to his age and understanding, and ensure that his wishes and feelings are communicated to the court. The guardian ad litem's over-riding duty is to advise the court as to what is in the best interests of the child. The guardian ad litem presents to the court an independent view in proceedings where critical decisions may be made about a child's future. Courts are likely to rely heavily on her advice and opinion.

---

4   Guardians ad litem and Reporting Officers (Panels) Regulations 1991, (SI 1991/2051).
5   See FPC (CA 1989) R 1991, r 10(7) and FPR 1991, r 4.10(7) for exclusions.
6   FPC (CA 1989) R 1991, r 10(1) and FPR 1991, r 4.10(1).

CHAPTER 2

APPOINTMENT OF GUARDIANS AD LITEM IN SPECIFIED PROCEEDINGS

Introduction

There is a presumption that a guardian ad litem will be appointed in all specified proceedings under the Children Act 1989. The Lord Chancellor[1] stated:

> "We accept that the courts are unlikely to find many cases in which it would be inappropriate to appoint a guardian ad litem".

Appointment

> *For the purpose of any specified proceedings, the court shall appoint a guardian ad litem for the child concerned, unless satisfied that it is not necessary to do so in order to safeguard his interests.*

> *(CA 1989 s 41(1))*

When appointing the guardian ad litem, the court or justices' clerk is required to consider appointing anyone who has acted as guardian ad litem in respect of the child in previous proceedings[2].

When the guardian ad litem has previously acted in respect of a parent who is also a minor, it would not normally be appropriate for the guardian ad litem to be appointed in respect of any child of that parent[3].

The guardian ad litem must be appointed as soon as practicable after the commencement of any proceedings[4], unless the justices' clerk or the court decides that the interests of the child can be safeguarded without the appointment of a guardian ad litem[5].

Where a guardian ad litem has not been appointed at the commencement of any proceedings, it is possible for her to be appointed at any time during those proceedings by the court[6] or on application by one of the parties. Where the justices' clerk or court does not grant such an application,

---

1   Hansard, HL, volume 503, col 408, quoted in Children Act Manual, Masson and Morris, 1992 p 123.
2   FPC (CA 1989) R 1991, r 10(8) and FPR 1991, r 4.10(8).
3   Practice Direction [1984] 1 All ER 69.
4   FPC (CA 1989) R 1991, r 10(1) and FPR 1991, r 4.10(1).
5   CA 1989 s 41(1).
6   FPC (CA 1989) R 1991, r 10(2),(4) and FPR 1991 r 4.10(2),(4).

reasons must be given and noted by the justices' clerk or proper officer of the court[7]. This decision may be the subject of an appeal.

Once the guardian ad litem is appointed, the justices' clerk or proper officer of the court must notify the guardian ad litem of her appointment and serve copies of the application and documents filed in the matter[8].

The *specified proceedings* for which a guardian ad litem may be appointed are contained in the Children Act 1989 and are as follows[9]:

- care or supervision order (section 31);
- a direction under section 37(1) for a local authority investigation of the child's circumstances where the court has made, or is considering whether to make, an interim care order (section 41(6)(b));
- discharge of a care order (section 39(1));
- variation or discharge of a supervision order (section 39(2));
- substitution of a supervision order for a care order (section 39(4));
- residence order where a child is the subject of a care order (section 8 and 91(1));
- contact with a child who is the subject of a care order (section 34);
- child assessment order (section 43);
- emergency protection order (section 44);
- variation of an emergency protection order (section 44 (9)(b));
- extension of an emergency protection order (section 45(4));
- discharge of an emergency protection order (section 45(8));
- recovery order (section 50);
- appeals (section 41(6)(h)).

Additional proceedings which are specified by the court rules to date are as follows[10]:

- secure accommodation order (section 25);
- changing the surname of a child in care (section 33(7));
- removing a child in care from the United Kingdom (section 33(7));
- permission for a child in care to live outside England and Wales (Schedule 2, paragraph 19(1));
- extension or further extension of a supervision order (Schedule 3, paragraph 6(3));
- appeals again the determination of proceedings specified in the court rules[11].

---

7   FPC (CA 1989) R 1991, r 10(3) and FPR 1991, r 4.10(3).
8   FPC (CA 1989) R 1991, r 10(6) and FPR 1991, r 4.10(6); for a description of the documents to be filed, see chapter 8 – Evidence.
9   CA 1989 s 41(6).
10   FPC (CA 1989) R 1991, r 2(2) and FPR 1991, r 4.2(2).
11   FPR 1991, r 4.2(2)(e) as inserted by Family Proceedings (Amendment) Rules 1991, (SI 1991/2113) reg 8.

Termination of appointment

The appointment of the guardian ad litem continues for the duration of the proceedings, unless otherwise directed by the court, or unless the appointment is terminated by the court[12].

Parties to any application may apply to terminate the appointment of a guardian ad litem, and the court is obliged to hear the views of the guardian ad litem and to give reasons in writing, when such an application is allowed[13]. A child may apply for leave to apply to terminate the appointment of the guardian ad litem and the guardian ad litem is entitled to make representations to the court.

Agent for the Official Solicitor

The Official Solicitor can ask a panel of guardians ad litem and reporting officers to provide a guardian ad litem to act as his agent[14]. A guardian ad litem acting as agent on behalf of the Official Solicitor carries out the duties requested by the Official Solicitor and not those of the guardian ad litem as described in this guide.

> *Where the guardian ad litem is the Official Solicitor, paragraph 2(a) shall not require him to appoint a solicitor for the child if he intends to act as the child's solicitor in the proceedings, unless –*
>
> *(a) the child wishes to instruct a solicitor direct; and*
> *(b) the Official Solicitor or the court considers that he is of sufficient understanding to do so.*
>
> *(FPR 1991, r 4.11(2A))[15]*

The Official Solicitor is not appointed to act in the magistrates' court and therefore is not able to act in children's cases in the family proceedings court.

The Official Solicitor usually only acts as guardian ad litem for a child who is the subject of applications in public law proceedings in the High Court. He does not accept appointment in county courts, (as a guardian ad litem from a panel of guardians ad litem and reporting officers will usually already have been appointed). The Official Solicitor has no capacity to act in the family proceedings court. The Official Solicitor may act as guardian ad litem for a child who is the subject of an application to the High Court under its inherent jurisdiction[16]. The Official Solicitor may act as guardian ad litem and solicitor, although a child of sufficient understanding may, with the court's leave, instruct his own solicitor.

---

12   FPC (CA 1989) R 1991, r 10(9) and FPR 1991, r 4.10(9).
13   FPC (CA 1989) R 1991, r 10(10) and FPR 1991, r 4.10(10).
14   [1991] 2 FLR 471; see appendix 1 for further details regarding the Official Solicitor's functions.
15   There is no equivalent rule in FPC (CA 1989) R 1991.
16   The High Court's inherent jurisdiction is its residual power to safeguard the welfare of the child in circumstances not otherwise provided for in CA 1989.

The Official Solicitor cannot be appointed for the child if he has acted for a parent of the child or if he is acting for any other party in the proceedings[17].

---

17   A v B and Hereford and Worcester County Council [1986] 1 FLR 289.

CHAPTER 3
POWERS AND DUTIES OF THE GUARDIAN AD LITEM

Introduction

The guardian ad litem shall –

(a) be appointed in accordance with rules of court; and

(b) be under a duty to safeguard the interests of the child in the manner prescribed by such rules.

(CA 1989 s 41(2))

The guardian ad litem's powers and duties are set out in rule 11 of the Family Proceedings Court (Children Act 1989) Rules 1991 and rule 4.11 of the Family Proceedings Rules 1991. The Rules emphasise the role of the guardian ad litem as an independent professional, and as the court's adviser regarding child care matters. The Rules allow the guardian ad litem to be consulted throughout the proceedings. The court must take account of the guardian ad litem's advice and recommendations. Where the court does not follow the recommendations of the guardian ad litem, it must give its reasons[1]. In most cases failure to give reasons for not following the guardian ad litem's recommendation will provide grounds for appeal[2].

Conduct of guardian ad litem's duties

In carrying out his duty under section 41(2), the guardian ad litem shall have regard to the principle set out in section 1(2) and the matters set out in section 1(3)(a) to (f) as if for the word "court" in that section there were substituted the words "guardian ad litem".

(FPC (CA 1989) R 1991, r 11(1))[3]

The matters set out in section 1(3) are known as the welfare check-list[4]. The court is asked to consider, additionally, section 1(3)(g), namely *the range and powers available to the court under this Act in the proceedings in question*, whereas the guardian ad litem is required by this rule to advise on *the options available to it* (the court) *in respect of the child and the suitability of each such option including what order should be made in determining the application*[5].

---

1   Re W (A minor) (Secure Accommodation Order) [1993] 1 FLR 692.
2   S v Oxfordshire [1993] 1 FLR 452; and also Devon County Council v Glancy [1985] 1 FLR 20.
3   FPR 1991, r 4.11(1).
4   The welfare checklist is set out on page 120 of this guide.
5   FPC (CA 1989) R 1991, r 11(4)(e) and FPR 1991, r 4.11(4)(e).

Appointment of solicitor

> *The guardian ad litem shall –*
>
> *(a) appoint a solicitor to represent the child, unless such a solicitor has already been appointed, and*
>
> *(b) give such advice to the child as is appropriate having regard to his understanding and, subject to rule 12(1)(a), instruct the solicitor representing the child on all matters relevant to the interests of the child, including possibilities for appeal, arising in the course of the proceedings.*
>
> *(FPC (CA 1989) R 1991, r 11(2))*[6]

The guardian ad litem normally appoints the solicitor for the child.

The court may appoint a solicitor. This may happen where a guardian ad litem is not available initially[7]. Where the child can and wishes to instruct his own solicitor the Rules provide for appointment by the court. By allowing the court the option to appoint a solicitor for the child, the Rules ensure that the child has legal representation when the proceedings begin, thus safeguarding his interests.

The guardian ad litem may apply to the court to dispense with the solicitor's services if the guardian ad litem feels it is appropriate to do so. She must be prepared to give her reasons; the child's solicitor, and a child of sufficient understanding, will be given the opportunity to make representations[8].

The guardian ad litem is responsible for instructing the solicitor for the child unless the child is judged by the solicitor to be able to give instructions on his own behalf[9] and there is a conflict between the guardian ad litem's instructions and any instructions the child might wish to give.

Where the guardian ad litem is instructing the child's solicitor, the guardian ad litem is responsible for informing the child, if of sufficient understanding about the proceedings[10], of the outcome of the final hearing and whether to lodge an appeal.

Child giving instructions to solicitor

> *Where it appears to the guardian ad litem that the child –*
>
> *(a) is instructing his solicitor direct, or*
>
> *(b) intends to, and is capable of, conducting the proceedings on his own behalf, he shall so inform the court through the justices' clerk and thereafter –*

---

6 FPR 1991, r 4.11(2).
7 CA 1989 s 41(3),(4).
8 FPC (CA 1989) R 1991, r 12(4) and FPR 1991, r 4.12(4).
9 FPC (CA 1989) R 1991, r 12(1)(a), r 11(3) and FPR 1991, r 4.12(1)(a), r 4.11(3); see chapter 6 – Legal representation.
10 FPC (CA 1989) R 1991, r 11(8) and FPR 1991, r 4.11(8).

> (i) *shall perform all of his duties set out in this rule, other than duties under paragraph (2)(a) and such other duties as the justices' clerk or the court may direct,*
>
> (ii) *shall take such part in the proceedings as the justices' clerk or the court may direct, and*
>
> (iii) *may, with leave of the justices' clerk or the court, have legal representation in his conduct of those duties.*
>
> > *(FPC (CA 1989) R 1991, r 11(3))*[11]

The solicitor can only take instructions from the child if he is of the opinion that the child is of sufficient understanding and capable of giving instructions independently. In this situation the solicitor must take instructions from the child. The guardian ad litem should be alert, at as early a stage as possible in the proceedings, to the possibility of conflict between her instructions and those of the child and bring it to the attention of the court. It is for the court ultimately to rule on the child's capacity to instruct a solicitor[12].

If the instructions of the child conflict with the opinion of the guardian ad litem, a direction may be made by the court that the guardian ad litem should have separate legal representation either upon application by the guardian ad litem or by the court itself upon its own motion. The legal aid rules prevent the guardian ad litem from receiving legal aid to fund her separate representation[13].

The guardian ad litem who seeks separate legal representation in her own right should apply to the court for a direction that she be separately represented and to her panel manager for funding of the representation by the local authority. The Regulations[14] state:

> *Each local authority shall defray the reasonable expenses incurred in respect of relevant proceedings by members of the panel established in respect of their area and pay fees and allowances for members of such panels in respect of relevant proceedings.*

Department of Health guidance[15] states:

> "a GALRO who seeks separate legal representation is not eligible for legal aid . . . and the local authority is liable to meet the costs."

---

11   FPR 1991, r 4.11(3).
12   Re M (Minors) (Care Proceedings: Child's Wishes) [1994] 1 FLR 749; 1 FCR 866.
13   Legal Aid Act 1988, s 15(3A)(c), as inserted by SI 1991/2036.
14   Guardian ad Litem and Reporting Officers (Panels) Regulations 1991 (SI 1991/2051) reg 9(1).
15   CA 1989 Guidance and Regulations vol 7: Guardians ad Litem and other Court Related Issues, para 2.36, p 9.

Directions appointments and hearings

The guardian ad litem shall, unless excused by the justices' clerk or the court, attend all directions appointments in, and hearings of, the proceedings and shall advise the justices' clerk or the court on the following matters –

(a) *whether the child is of sufficient understanding for any purpose including the child's refusal to submit to a medical or psychiatric examination or other assessment that the court has the power to require, direct or order;*

(b) *the wishes of the child in respect of any matter relevant to the proceedings, including his attendance at court;*

(c) *the appropriate forum for the proceedings;*

(d) *the appropriate timing of the proceedings or any part of them;*

(e) *the options available to it in respect of the child and the suitability of each such option including what order should be made in determining the application;*

(f) *any other matter concerning which the justices' clerk or the court seeks his advice or concerning which he considers that the court should be informed.*

(FPC (CA 1989) R 1991, r 11(4))[16]

Although the guardian ad litem is expected to attend all directions appointments and give her advice orally or in writing[17], she may be involved in another case, in another court, or there may be some other pressing reason why her attendance is either not possible or should be curtailed[18]. In such circumstances, it will be necessary to contact the court and ask either for permission to be excused from the directions appointment or for its date or time to be changed. Where the guardian ad litem is unable to attend, the court may be assisted by having the guardian ad litem's input in writing, with copies being sent to all other parties. The guardian ad litem must ensure that the solicitor for the child is fully informed, instructed and in a position to advise the court on her behalf.

Directions appointments focus on preparing the case for the final hearing and the court relies heavily on the guardian ad litem's advice. The court will expect the guardian ad litem to advise it on such matters as:

- the wishes and feelings of the child, taking into account the child's understanding and maturity;
- the child's attendance at court hearings;
- whether the child has sufficient understanding to give consent to a medical examination, psychiatric or any other assessment;
- the need for, and the relevant disciplines of, expert evidence.

---

16   FPR 1991, r 4.11(4).
17   FPC (CA 1989) R 1991 r 11(5) and FPR 1991 r 4.11(5).
18   The Children Act Advisory Committee Report 1992/3 LCD p 65–66.

The court will expect the guardian ad litem and the child's solicitor to have considered whether or not the proceedings are in the appropriate court, and whether (amongst other factors) the complexity, gravity, importance or urgency of the case, or the need to consolidate it with other matters, require it to be transferred from the family proceedings court to the county court, or to the High Court[19]. Consideration should also be given as to whether delay might be avoided in hearing the matter if it were transferred laterally within the same tier of courts to a less busy court. If the criteria leading to an upwards transfer no longer apply[20], consideration should be given by the guardian ad litem and the child's solicitor as to whether to recommend transfer back to a lower court. Decisions about transfer should be taken as soon as possible to avoid delaying the final hearing.

The need for a particular assessment or the complexities of the case may require a delay in the final hearing to allow time for their completion. The guardian ad litem will need to demonstrate how any such delay would be in the child's interest – so called "constructive delay".

Where there are criminal proceedings in which there is evidence relevant to the care proceedings, a child's interests may require the civil case to be heard before the criminal case because further delay would be contrary to the child's best interests. On the other hand, if there are grounds for expediting the hearing of the criminal case so that the civil case can be heard immediately thereafter, then the guardian ad litem should consider applying to the court for a direction that a request be made to the criminal listing office for the expedited hearing of the criminal matter.

The options available in respect of the child and the suitability of each option are matters about which the guardian ad litem will advise the court orally as well as in the text of her final report. Compilation of her report is the guardian ad litem's principal task. The purpose of the report is to *"advise on the interests of the child"*. There is no prescribed format, and it is left to the individual guardian ad litem to determine the content and layout[21].

At directions appointments or hearings, the court may ask the advice of the guardian ad litem about the appropriateness of making further interim orders. The local authority may have filed an interim care plan; the guardian ad litem should be prepared to consider this and offer an opinion to the court on the plan[22]. The guardian ad litem will be required to comment on whether it is appropriate that a child be placed in local authority care, his own home or the home of relatives for the duration of the proceedings.

---

19 Children (Allocation of Proceedings) Order (SI 1991/1677), art 7(1)(a),(b),(c); see chapter 9 – Directions appointments and hearings.

20 Children (Allocation of Proceedings) Order (SI 1991/1677), art 11 & 13.

21 Guardians ad litem should ascertain whether their local family court's business committees have issued any local guidance regarding report formats; see chapter 4 – Guardian ad litem's investigation and report.

The court may ask the guardian ad litem about any particular point or matter that the court believes the guardian ad litem can advise upon. Equally, the guardian ad litem is allowed to comment, without being asked by the court, upon any matters she believes to be relevant and should be put before the court at a directions appointment[22] or interim hearings.

Advice given to the court

The advice given under paragraph (4) may, subject to any order of the court, be given orally or in writing; and if the advice be given orally, a note of it shall be taken by the justices' clerk or the court.

(FPC (CA 1989) R 1991, r 11(5))[23]

The guardian ad litem should make herself available to advise the court at directions appointments or hearings either orally[24] or in writing[25]. The guardian ad litem may be required to present an interim report in writing for a directions appointment or an interim hearing[25].

Advising possible parties

The guardian ad litem shall, where practicable, notify any person whose joinder as a party to those proceedings would be likely, in the guardian ad litem's opinion, to safeguard the interests of the child, of that person's right to apply to be joined under rule 7(2) and shall inform the justices' clerk or the court –

(a) of any such notification given,
(b) of anyone whom he attempted to notify under this paragraph but was unable to contact, and
(c) of anyone whom he believes may wish to be joined to the proceedings.

(FPC (CA 1989) R 1991, r 11(6))[26]

The guardian ad litem is expected to notify any prospective party of his right to apply to be joined to the proceedings, where she believes that this would be appropriate to safeguard the interests of the child. Possible parties might include a father who does not have parental responsibility, step-parents, grandparents, siblings or other members of the extended family. The guardian ad litem is advised to refer any possible party to the panel of solicitors who act in children cases published by the Law Society[27].

---

22   FPC (CA 1989) R 1991, r 11(4)(f) and FPR 1991 r 4.11(4)(f).
23   FPR 1991, r 4.11(5).
24   See chapter 8 – Evidence, regarding oral evidence.
25   Hampshire CC v S [1993] 1 FLR 559; see chapter 10 – Interim hearings, for advice about interim reports; see also chapter 18 – Interim care and supervision orders.
26   FPR 1991, r 4.11(6).
27   Children Panel – Law Society, 113 Chancery Lane, London WC2A 1PL; see also chapter 6 – Legal representation.

Filing a report

> *The guardian ad litem shall, unless the justices' clerk or the court otherwise directs, not less than seven days before the date fixed for the final hearing of the proceedings, file a written report advising on the interests of the child; and the justices' clerk shall, as soon as practicable, serve a copy of the reports on the parties.*
>
> *(FPC (CA 1989) R 1991, r 11(7))*[28]

The guardian ad litem is required by the rules to file her report seven days before the final hearing, or as otherwise directed by the court. The court must send a copy of the report to the parties to the proceedings. This is likely to result in parties receiving the report, at best, less than seven days before the final hearing. Directions should be sought from the court regarding the filing of the guardian ad litem's report and its service. The court may wish to specify an earlier filing date so that a copy can be sent to all parties seven days before the hearing, or to direct the guardian ad litem to serve the report directly upon the parties.

If the guardian ad litem and the child's solicitor believe a particular piece of information should not be disclosed to one of the parties, an application should be made to the court for an appropriate direction. The court will not sanction non-disclosure unless it is "fully satisfied judicially that real harm" will come to the child by disclosure: a risk of significant harm is not enough[29].

Acceptance of service of documents

> *The guardian ad litem shall serve and accept service of documents on behalf of the child in accordance with rule 8(3)(b) and (4)(b) and, where the child has not himself been served, and has sufficient understanding, advise the child of the contents of any document so served.*
>
> *(FPC (CA 1989) R 1991, r 11(8))*[30]

The guardian ad litem shall accept service of documents on behalf of the child where no solicitor represents the child[31]. The guardian ad litem is entitled to be served separately with all documents and statements[32]. Where the child has a solicitor, his solicitor will accept service of documents and also serve documents on behalf of the child. The guardian ad litem has a duty to advise the child as to the contents of such documents served upon him, subject to the child having sufficient understanding to comprehend the nature of the documents[33]. Depending on the child's understanding and

---

28 FPR 1991, r 4.11(7).
29 Re M (Minors)(Disclosure of Evidence) [1994] 1 FLR 760.
30 FPR 1991, r 4.11(8).
31 FPC (CA 1989) R 1991, r 8(3)(b) and FPR 1991, r 4.8(3)(b).
32 FPC (CA 1989) R 1991, r 17(1) and FPR 1991, r 4.17(1).
33 FPC (CA 1989) R 1991, r 11(8) and FPR 1991 r 4.11(8).

whether the child is instructing the solicitor, the solicitor may advise the child with regard to the contents of any document served upon him[34].

Investigation

The guardian ad litem shall make such investigations as may be necessary for him to carry out his duties and shall, in particular –

(a) contact or seek to interview such persons as he thinks appropriate or as the court directs,

(b) if he inspects records of the kinds referred to in section 42, bring to the attention of the court, through the justices' clerk, and such other persons as the justices' clerk or the court may direct, all such records and documents which may, in his opinion, assist in the proper determination of the proceedings, and

(c) obtain such professional assistance as is available to him which he thinks appropriate or which the justices' clerk or the court directs him to obtain."

(FPC (CA 1989) R 1991, r 11(9))[35]

The guardian ad litem may interview whoever she believes may be relevant to the investigation[36], or such persons as the court directs, provided the person concerned is willing to be interviewed. If a particular individual, whom the guardian ad litem believes could provide important information that would assist her investigation, refuses to be interviewed by the guardian ad litem, the refusal should be mentioned at a directions appointment or hearing. If sufficiently important, the court could issue a witness summons or a summons to produce documents to the court.

The guardian ad litem must consider whether any documents contained within local authority records should be placed before the court to assist it in the proper determination of the proceedings. The duty of the guardian ad litem extends to satisfying herself that the local authority's statements fairly reflect the matters contained in the records. The guardian ad litem has the right to examine and take copies of documents[37] held by the local authority regarding the child, including documents about prospective placements[38].

The guardian ad litem should seek a direction from the court if she wishes to see any related court files.

Whilst the guardian ad litem does not have the right to examine hospital or doctors' records or records of other agencies, she should consider raising the refusal of any such agency to allow access at a directions appointment.

---

34   FPC (CA 1989) R 1991, r 12(2) and FPR 1991, r 4.12(2).

35   FPR 1991, r 4.11(9).

36   See chapter 4 – The guardian ad litem's investigation and report.

37   CA 1989 s 42(1),(2).

38   Re T (A Minor) (Guardian ad Litem: Case Record) [1994] 1 FLR 632.

Subject to her obtaining the court's permission[39], the guardian ad litem may instruct, or request the child's solicitor to instruct, professionals to carry out assessments, whether they be medical, psychiatric, psychological or any other type of assessment that is needed[40]. Prior authority for the funding of such an assessment should usually be obtained from the Legal Aid Board by the child's solicitor. The Legal Aid Board will not fund any assessment which it considers should be the responsibility of the local authority.

Other assistance

In addition to his duties under other paragraphs of this rule, the guardian ad litem shall provide to the justices' clerk or the court such other assistance as it may require.

(FPC (CA 1989) R 1991, r 11(10))[41]

The court has the power to give the guardian ad litem specific instructions regarding any aspects of the case and direct the guardian ad litem to provide any other assistance as it may require, such as advice about a child's cultural or religious background or intra-familial contact.

Right of parties to question the guardian ad litem

A party may question the guardian ad litem about oral or written advice tendered by him to the justices' clerk or the court under this rule.

(FPC (CA 1989) R 1991, r 11(11))[42]

The guardian ad litem must be ready to be cross-examined about any evidence or advice she places before the court.

Local authority

The guardian ad litem should be consulted by the local authority when it is taking any major case decisions throughout the period of the guardian ad litem's appointment. The local authority should ascertain the guardian ad litem's views about any proposals that would bring about a significant change in the child's circumstances[43].

The local authority has a duty to consult the guardian ad litem before taking any decision to remove a child from a foster parent during the currency of any proceedings[44]. The local authority cannot withdraw an application for a care or supervision order without leave of the court, which must allow the guardian ad litem an opportunity to make representations[45].

---

39   FPC (CA 1989) R 1991, r 18(1) and FPR 1991, r 4.18(1).
40   See chapter 9 – Directions appointments and hearings.
41   FPR 1991, r 4.11(10).
42   FPR 1991, r 4.11(11).
43   R v North Yorkshire County Council ex parte M [1989] 1 FLR 203.
44   R v Hereford and Worcester County Council ex parte D [1992] 1 FLR 448.
45   FPC (CA 1989) R 1991, r 5(1),(4)(a) and FPR 1991, r 4.5(1),(4)(a).

Summary

The guardian ad litem's chief value to the court is as an experienced professional with independent judgment. She is given the scope to carry out investigations as she thinks appropriate within the boundaries of the legislative framework. The guardian ad litem takes an overview of the case which is invaluable to the court and child. She has the power and duty to consider all aspects of the case and all the arguments that are put before the court. With all this information she is in a strong position to formulate her conclusions and make recommendations to the court about how best to safeguard the welfare of the child.

PART 2

THE GUARDIAN AD LITEM'S INVESTIGATION AND REPORT

CHAPTER 4

THE GUARDIAN AD LITEM'S INVESTIGATION AND REPORT

Introduction

This chapter describes matters which should be contained in the guardian ad litem's report in care proceedings under section 31. The report structure can be adapted to suit other applications. Specific advice about the guardian ad litem's investigation and report in the other specified proceedings is provided separately in this guide in the chapters relating to each application[1].

The Department of Health has published two guides that cover in detail the guardian ad litem's investigation and social work assessment. They are:

- Manual of Practice Guidance for Guardians ad Litem and Reporting Officers (particularly part II)[2]; and
- Protecting Children: A Guide for Social Workers undertaking a Comprehensive Assessment[3].

This chapter should be read in conjunction with these guides.

Initial appointment

The court wishing to appoint[4] a guardian ad litem will obtain the name of an available guardian ad litem from the panel manager or administrator. Written notification[5] of the appointment will be sent to all the parties and the guardian ad litem will also receive copies of the application and of any other papers submitted to the court.

The guardian ad litem should check that the papers she receives are correct and that the necessary information is supplied. The forms will include:

- the name of the child;
- the application;
- the grounds for the application;
- whether or not a solicitor has been appointed;
- details of the child's family;
- details of those with parental responsibility;

---

1   See chapters 13 – 25.
2   HMSO, 1992.
3   HMSO, 1988.
4   See chapter 1 – Introduction, and chapter 2 – Appointment of guardian ad litem.
5   Form C47.

- proposals for contact;
- outline of the plan for the child should the order applied for be made.

When the guardian ad litem is satisfied that she has sufficient information and that the application concerns specified proceedings, she should proceed to appoint a solicitor to represent the child and commence her investigation.

Investigation

The guardian ad litem's involvement is limited to the duration of the proceedings and because of its very nature, must be task-centred; the objective is to collect and assimilate as much relevant information as possible in order to advise and prepare a report for the court in the best interests of the child.

The guardian ad litem should interview or speak to all those whom she believes will be able to contribute to her understanding of the case, including parents and relevant members of the extended family, as well as members of agencies involved with the child and his family. She may interview individuals or professionals more than once. She may ask the parties if they wish a particular individual to be interviewed. The court may direct the guardian ad litem to attempt to interview a specific person or member of the family or address specific issues[6]. When interviewing, the guardian ad litem should prepare notes of each interview at the time or soon after and bear in mind that these could form part of the evidence at a hearing[7].

The child should be observed, where relevant, with his parents/carers, siblings, other family members, foster parents and perhaps in his nursery or school. The guardian ad litem must decide how detailed her enquiries should be. Below is a list of areas the guardian ad litem should cover in the course of her enquiries:

- interview parents and other adults who are important to child, or who have been involved in his care[6];
- interview any siblings;
- interview members of the extended family, where relevant[6];
- interview professionals involved in the case, e.g. social worker, health visitor, general practitioner, school teacher, foster parents[6];
- instruction of expert if appropriate[8];
- inspect local authority records (social services and education)[9];
- whether the child is having contact or sufficient contact with parents, grandparents and siblings;
- the likely date when the case will be ready for hearing (timetabling)[10];

---

6   FPC (CA 1989) R 1991, r 11(9)(a) and FPR 1991, r 4.11(9)(a).
7   See chapter 8 – Evidence.
8   FPC (CA 1989) R 1991, r 11(9)(c) and FPR 1991, r 4.11(9)(c); see chapter 7 – Expert reports.
9   FPC (CA 1989) R 1991, r 11(9)(b) and FPR 1991, r 4.11(9)(b); see chapter 8 – Evidence.
10   See chapter 9 – Directions appointments and hearings.

- whether further directions hearings are necessary[11];
- consultation with solicitor to evaluate evidence[12];
- whether the order sought is appropriate and whether the statutory are criteria met[13];
- whether there is a possibility of conflict between the views of the guardian ad litem and those of the child.

At the end of her investigations, the guardian ad litem should be in a position to:

- advise the court of the facts of the case;
- confirm that she has spoken to or otherwise has written information from, all those relevant to the proceedings;
- present a clear understanding of the wishes and feelings of the child;
- present an assessment of the child's needs;
- appraise the actions of the local authority;
- comment on the care plan;
- evaluate the options available to the court;
- make a recommendation to the court with regard to disposal.

Preparation of the report

The guardian ad litem's report will be read by the parties (possibly the child), social workers, court clerks, magistrates, legal representatives, expert witnesses and the judge. With such a range of readers it is essential that the report is readable for all those who will see it.

The report should avoid jargon and phrases or words which are not easily understood by the lay person. The report should be written in clear, correct and concise English. It must differentiate between professional opinion, undisputed and disputed facts of the case. The layout should make it easy to read.

In order to assist the reader of the report and enable notes to be made in the margins for the purpose of cross examination by solicitors or barristers, and note taking by magistrates, judges or parties the following practical suggestions may be helpful:

- a title page including court number;
- a contents page;
- wide margins;
- double spacing;
- numbered paragraphs;
- all headings in bold type;
- use one side only of paper;
- ensure the report is signed and dated (this is essential because the court need not otherwise accept the report).

---

11 See chapter 9 – Directions appointments and hearings.
12 See chapter 6 – Legal representation.
13 See chapters 13 – 25 for further information about each order.

The report should be lodged with the court at least seven days prior to the final hearing[14], unless a direction is made that the report should be filed earlier.

The report

The report is a free-standing document. Its purpose is to describe in clear and unambiguous terms (referring where necessary to other documents before the court), the enquiries undertaken, the background to the case, the child's views (if appropriate), an assessment of the child's needs and a recommendation with regard to disposal, as well as a discussion of the options available to the court.

The guardian ad litem should be careful not to venture outside her own area of expertise as a social worker in the giving of opinion and assessments. She should seek expert advice on the interpretation of controversial material expecially in regard to allegations of sexual abuse[15].

The issue as to whether abuse has occurred is for the court, not the guardian ad litem, to decide. The guardian ad litem should present to the court a fair and balanced assessment of the factors which seem to her to be material and point in either direction, basing her recommendations on alternative premises, namely whether a finding of abuse is to be made or not[15].

The guardian ad litem is likely to be cross-examined upon the contents of her report. It must refer to all the issues and be balanced in its observations; it is for the court to make decisions with regard to the disposal of the case. It is essential all the facts and arguments are placed before the court so that it is able to make an informed decision. It is good practice, where possible, to include in the report only matters which have been discussed with the parties beforehand.

In cases involving sibling groups consideration will have to be given to whether a composite report with separate sections for each child or separate reports should be prepared. A composite report will have the advantage of avoiding unnecessary repetition but there may be cases where separate reports may be preferable, particularly where significantly different care plans are being contemplated.

---

14   FPC (CA 1989) R 1991, r 11(7) and FPR 1991, r 4.11(7).
15   B v B (Procedure: Alleged Sexual Abuse) [1994] 1 FCR 809.

The following format may need to be adapted by individual guardians ad litem to suit any application in specified proceedings. The structure will need to reflect the particular circumstances of each case:

- Front sheet;
- Information about the application(s);
- Contents of report;
- Experience and qualifications of guardian ad litem;
- Summary of case;
- Summary of previous court hearings;
- Enquiries undertaken;
- Family structure;
- Background history;
- Parents;
- Other relevant adults;
- The child;
- Any significant harm suffered or likely to be suffered by the child;
- Wishes and feelings of the child;
- Expert assessments and professionals interviewed;
- Local authority care plan;
- Summary (including welfare check-list);
- Contact;
- Options available to the court;
- Recommendations;
- Signature and date.

A description of each section is presented below.

Front sheet

The front sheet should identify the report, the case and the panel, but avoid providing any more information in order to provide maximum confidentiality. Reference to confidentiality is essential to guard against misuse of the report.

CASE NO.

NAME OF COURT

GUARDIAN AD LITEM REPORT

Date of report

CONFIDENTIAL

**NAME OF PANEL OF GUARDIANS AD LITEM
AND REPORTING OFFICERS**

This report has been prepared for the court and should be treated as confidential. It must not be shown, nor its contents revealed, to any person other than a party to the proceedings or a legal adviser to such a party without leave of the court.

Information about the application(s)

This section should provide basic information about the application.

		Case No.
Subject: Name of child(ren)	**dob**	**age**
Type of Proceedings:	Children Act 1989	
Application for:	List of applications and relevant section of Children Act 1989	
Date of hearing:		
Guardian ad litem:		
Appointment date:		
Solicitor for the child:		

Contents of report

All sections of the report should be listed to enable easy reference for the reader, and quick reference for all parties during the hearing. Guardians ad litem may feel that this is not necessary for short reports.

Experience and qualifications of guardian ad litem

The guardian ad litem should give her academic and professional qualifications and her experience. She should also say how long she has been practising as a guardian ad litem.

Summary of the case

A brief outline of the causes of concern which led to the proceedings being commenced, and the orders being sought by the different parties should be presented. This section should indicate who has parental responsibility in respect of the child.

Summary of previous court hearings

In some cases it may be useful to have a list of hearings, date of transfer and summary of directions; however this is not necessary if they are clearly listed and summarised elsewhere in the court papers.

Enquiries undertaken

This section details the basis of the report and the information upon which the guardian ad litem's assessment has been based. It will be of particular assistance when the guardian ad litem is giving evidence and being cross-examined.

I have interviewed the following people:

Name   Relationship to child   Date(s)

I have interviewed by telephone the following people:

Name   Relationship to child   Date(s)

Documents read/evidence seen:

Report of   Date of report
Statement of   Date of statement
Video recording of   Date of recording
Case files   Date

Where the guardian ad litem has not seen or been able to contact a person who is particularly relevant to the proceedings, the reason could be stated in this section.

Family Structure

The family structure should include all the key people in the child's family, their relationship to the child and whether the parents are married. A format for a simple family structure is suggested below:

Relationship to subject of report	Name	DOB/Age	Address
Mother			
Father			
Subject			
Brother			
Sister			
Co-habitees			
Relatives			

In many cases where there are complicated family structures and relationships, it will be necessary to produce a genogram (family tree) to explain in diagrammatic form the structure of the family. This is often found by the courts to be very helpful. Guidance on preparing genograms can be found in "Protecting Children: A Guide for Social Workers undertaking a Comprehensive Assessment"[16].

Background history

The background history is distinct from the chronology usually provided to the court by the applicant. Its purpose is to describe the family history relevant to the events which gave rise to the application before the court.

This should include:

- a history of the parents, including any abuse suffered, family breakdown, standards of care experienced as a child, illness, periods spent in local authority care and relevant convictions;
- a history of the children, including birth, abuse, family breakdown, care arrangements, illness, involvement of social services, and child protection conferences.

Parents

This section should provide an assessment of the child's parents with a view to identifying whether they can care for their child, and if so, whether any changes in their parenting need to be made.

---

16   HMSO, 1988 p 81.

The term 'parent' may include any step-parent, cohabitee or other carer. Such an assessment needs to include the following:

- Parents' history:
  including (where relevant) a broader chronological account of the parents' history than that provided in the background history section; the parents' experiences as children, any abuse they suffered, their medical and any psychiatric histories; and any criminal convictions.

- Parents' views:
  including the parents' understanding of their own history and experience and its impact upon their ability to parent the child; the parents' respective views regarding the child's interests, welfare and needs and their attitude towards the application, and the issues raised in the proceedings; the parents' account of, and attitude towards, any injuries or abuse and whether they take any responsibility for it.

- Observation of parents:
  including observations made by the guardian ad litem of the parents as individuals; how they respond to questions, their affect, individual abilities and understanding.

- Family observations:
  including information about relationships between the parents; the quality of those relationships; a description of the atmosphere that might be experienced by the child within the family; parents' communication patterns and ability to set boundaries within the family; any observations from contact between the child and parent regarding the parent; and a description of the parents' respective relationships with the child.

- Parents' capacities:
  including the capacities of the parents to care for the child; to provide a home for the child; their intellectual capacity; employment circumstances; ability to provide physically for the child; the style of their parenting, including how controlling the parent might be; their understanding of the child and his needs; how responsive they are to the child; the extent to which the parents might be preoccupied with their own needs and therefore neglectful of the child; and the parents' capacity for change.

Other relevant adults

Depending on the relevance of other adults to the child, this may require one or several sections. Grandparents and other relatives who may have been caring for the child, or who seek to care for the child, should be assessed in a similar manner to that outlined above for the parents.

Family members may have views to offer about any harm suffered by the child, where the child should be placed or any other aspect of the application.

The child

The guardian ad litem should include her own observations and assessment; and detail the basis upon which the assessment was made; and consider the assessments of the child made by other professionals and on what basis they were made. Any research referred to or used by the guardian ad litem needs to be clearly referenced. Where a composite report is being prepared involving more than one child, there should be separate sections on each child.

The guardian ad litem should be able to present and demonstrate to the court a comprehensive understanding of the child's needs – physical, psychological, educational, health, development and attachments – given his age and maturity. This section should describe the child's gender, race, culture, religion, language and any disability the child may suffer; and discuss their implications for the child's welfare and interests.

Any significant harm suffered or likely to be suffered by the child

In care or supervision order applications[17] the threshold criteria should be considered critically in respect of each child. This may require separate sections for each child in composite reports. Any significant harm suffered by the child or likely to be suffered should be described. The guardian ad litem should be mindful that "*harm" means ill treatment or the impairment of health or development*[18]. Harm should be analysed in terms of:

■ any ill treatment suffered by the child, which includes sexual abuse and forms of ill treatment which are not physical;

■ any impairment of health of the child, which means physical or mental health;

■ any impairment of development of the child, which means physical, intellectual, emotional, social or behavioural development.

In considering the harm suffered by the child the guardian ad litem will need to explain, in so far as it is possible, the cause of the harm.

The child's wishes and feelings

The guardian ad litem should include in her report a specific section dealing with the wishes and feelings of the child, or of each child in composite reports. The weight attached to the child's views by the court will depend on the age and understanding of the child and should be discussed in this section. It is important that any view expressed by the child is included in the report as well as any relevant comments made by the child. It may be appropriate to record the exact words that the child used, provided that the context in which they were said is explained clearly and accurately. When

---

17   See chapter 17 – Care and supervision orders.
18   CA 1989 s 31(9).

seeking to ascertain the child's wishes and feelings, the guardian ad litem should, where possible, interview the child on his own.

The guardian ad litem must make the child's wishes and feelings, and how these were ascertained, known to the court[19]. In so far as it is possible, the guardian ad litem should try to avoid questions which could be construed as leading questions, i.e. questions which suggest the answer or which contain information in the question which could affect the answer. In any event, the expressed wishes and feelings may depend on the child's understanding of the options available to him, as well as the child's understanding of who will see the information. The court and other parties will be assisted by the guardian ad litem describing the sort of questions used, as well as the child's answers.

Older children may only be too well aware of the impact that revealing their wishes and feelings to the court might have on their parents and their parents' attitude towards them. To help establish whether the child feels able to talk freely, the guardian ad litem should first inform him that his views will not remain confidential and ascertain the child's views about this. The child's expressed wishes and feelings can be considered in the light of whether he has felt able to express them without inhibition.

It should be remembered that no matter how young, disabled or disturbed a child may be, he may still have ascertainable wishes and it is the guardian ad litem's duty to elicit these and present them to the court. Further, a child can express wishes and feelings through non-verbal communication. When interviewing the child the following points should be considered:

- the child should be helped to understand at an age-appropriate level, the role of the guardian ad litem and the reason for her visit prior to attempting to ascertain his wishes and feelings;
- the guardian ad litem should take into account the child's age, sex, ethnic background, stage of development and any other characteristics which she considers relevant;
- whether the child's first language is English and whether the services of an interpreter are required;
- the guardian ad litem should be aware of her own values and how they might influence her judgement;
- the guardian ad litem should remain as objective as possible and try to make the child aware of her objectivity;
- the guardian ad litem should interview at the child's pace;
- the guardian ad litem should not influence the child's responses;
- the guardian ad litem should take care not to misinterpret the responses given by the child.

The court will welcome advice from the guardian ad litem as to the weight that should be attached to the expression of a child's wishes in any individual case.

---

19   FPC (CA 1989) R 1991, r 11(4)(b) and FPR 1991, r 4.11(4)(b).

In representing what is in the child's best interests the guardian ad litem should take into account the child's physical, emotional and educational needs[20]. It may be helpful for the guardian ad litem to discuss with the child, in age-appropriate language, how he feels his best interests would be served with regard to his physical, emotional and educational needs. This is particularly relevant when dealing with an older child.

The guardian ad litem has to consider any harm which the child has suffered or is at risk of suffering[21]. She will want to consider very carefully the evidence regarding significant harm or the likelihood of significant harm. This is an area where it may be appropriate for the guardian ad litem to discuss with the child, depending on his age and understanding, his perception of the harm he has suffered or is likely to suffer in the future.

The child may well have an opinion about who is capable of meeting his needs[22] and of the likely effect on him of any change of his circumstances[23]. The guardian ad litem should try and elicit from the child, in so far as it is appropriate given his age and maturity, his views on these matters.

It is often extremely difficult to ascertain the child's views and, even when the child is articulating a clear view, he may still be too young to understand the reasons why he is the subject of court proceedings and the issues surrounding the case. The guardian ad litem should use her skill in communicating with the child, whether it be through play, use of written material or in discussion. The method used in communicating with him will depend upon the age of the child and his understanding. Where it is not appropriate or possible to probe the child directly regarding his ascertainable wishes and feelings, the guardian ad litem will have to rely on other evidence of the child's wishes and feelings such as views expressed to foster carers.

If the guardian ad litem experiences difficulty in communicating with the child, it may be appropriate for her to seek the advice of an expert. This would be particularly appropriate where the child suffers a disability, or is handicapped and has specific communication needs. Expertise in areas such as speech therapy or sign language may be required to facilitate communication. Legal aid should be sought to finance this. Where the child's first language is not English and an interpreter is required, funding should be sought from the panel.

The guardian ad litem has an obligation to include in her report and in her oral evidence the wishes and feelings of the child, irrespective of whether the guardian ad litem agrees with the child's views.

---

20   CA 1989 s 1(3)(b).
21   CA 1989 s 1(3)(e).
22   CA 1989 s 1(3)(f).
23   CA 1989 s 1(3)(c).

Expert assessments and professionals interviewed

This section will only be necessary where the views expressed in reports provided by any expert instructed by the guardian ad litem, the local authority or any other parties have not been included under the sections about the child, parents or other relevant adults. These reports may include psychiatric reports, psychological reports, paediatric assessments or the results of other medical examinations. The views of other professionals in the case who have not submitted a written report, but whom the guardian ad litem has interviewed may also be included in this section.

Local authority care plan

The guardian ad litem will be expected to scrutinise the local authority's care plan[24] [25] and, where appropriate, comment on the local authority's actions, both past and present. The guardian ad litem is likely to be the only independent child care professional in the case from the same discipline as the local authority workers involved. Accordingly, where she concludes that professional criticism must be made of past or intended future actions of the local authority, her views may be of particular value to the court. Where possible, evidence supporting the care plan should be made available to the court by the local authority[25]. When examining the care plan, the guardian ad litem should be aware of the contents of Department of Health guidance[26] which lists the key elements it should contain, and with which the care plan should accord so far as it is possible[27]:

- the child's identified needs (including needs arising from race, culture, religion or language, special educational or health needs);
- how those needs might be met;
- the aim of the plan and timescale; the proposed placement (type and details);
- other services to be provided to child and/or family;
- arrangements for contact and reunification;
- support in placement;
- likely duration of placement in the accommodation;
- contingency plan, if the placement breaks down;
- arrangements for ending the placement (if made under voluntary arrangements);
- who is to be responsible for implementing the plan (specific tasks and overall plan);
- specific detail of the parents' role in day-to-day arrangements;
- the extent to which the wishes and views of the child, his parents and anyone else with sufficient interest in the child (including representatives of other agencies) have been obtained and acted upon; the reasons supporting this course of action or explanations as to why these wishes and views have been discounted;

---

24   Re T (A Minor) (Care Order: Conditions) [1994] FLR 423.
25   Re J (Minors) (Care: Care Plan) [1994] 1 FLR 253.
26   CA 1989 Guidance and Regulations, vol 3 Family Placements para 2.62 p 15.
27   Manchester City Council v F [1993] 1 FLR 419.

- arrangements for input by parents, the child and others into the ongoing decision-making process;
- arrangements for notifying the responsible authority of disagreements or making representations;
- arrangements for health care (including consent to examination and treatment);
- arrangements for education;
- dates of reviews.

The guardian ad litem needs to consider what steps the local authority have taken to keep the family together as a family unit, and the services offered to them.

Summary, including the welfare check-list

At the conclusion of the report, based on the various assessments in each section of the report, those of the local authority and other professionals, the guardian ad litem should be in a position to:

- describe and explain the circumstances which resulted in the causes for concern which led to the application;
- where the causes for concern still can not be explained or understood, or where the facts are in dispute, the guardian ad litem should be able to indicate what has not been explained and/or not been understood, as well as the disputed facts in issue;
- describe the patterns of interaction and functioning within the family and between the adults;
- indicate whether during the course of the assessment any changes (positive and negative) have occurred within the individual parents or other relevant adults, their relationship with the child and/or relationships within the family;
- indicate whether any changes in the child have been perceived during the course of the guardian ad litem's investigation, and identify what factor(s) might have accounted for these changes;
- indicate whether any or all of the circumstances, which resulted in the causes for concern, still exist;
- indicate whether there are sufficient changes in the family functioning to contemplate the rehabilitation of the child;
- comment on the care plan.

The summary must balance the risks to the child of permanent or short term separation from his parents against any risks of significant harm, should he remain in, or be returned to, the care of his parent(s) or carer(s). Further guidance about the factors that need to be taken into account when balancing the risk to the child, can be found in chapter ten of "Protecting Children: A Guide for Social Workers undertaking a Comprehensive Assessment"[28].

---

28   HMSO 1988 p 75.

The welfare check-list[29] is provided to ensure that the court considers all relevant matters in reaching its decision. The welfare check-list[30] can be used where appropriate to structure the summary using each section as a subheading:

- the ascertainable wishes and feeling of the child concerned (considered in the light of his age and understanding);
- his physical, emotional and educational needs;
- the likely effect on him of any change of his circumstances;
- his age, sex, background and any characteristics of his which the court considers relevant;
- any harm which he has suffered or is at risk of suffering;
- how capable each of his parents, and any other person in relation to whom the court considers the question to be relevant, is of meeting his needs.

Contact

Before making a care order the court is required to consider the local authority's proposals for contact[31] and the views of other parties[32].

In care applications the guardian ad litem should consider whether to include a specific recommendation with regard to contact, remembering that when making a care order with respect to a child, or in any family proceedings where the child is the subject of a care order, the court can make a contact order even though no application has been made for that order.

Contact does not necessarily have to be face-to-face contact but may take the form of indirect contact such as written or telephone communication or the provision of photographs. Contact in the form of overnight stays may be appropriate, especially if rehabilitation is being considered.

The guardian ad litem must outline the aim, purpose, frequency and type of contact and with whom it is to take place, i.e. parents, siblings, grandparents, or others. She should then state how the proposed contact is going to meet the child's needs, both now and in the future, and whether it is part of a rehabilitation plan.

Caution should be exercised to avoid establishing inflexible arrangements that may become unsuitable as the child grows older. Changing these arrangements will require an application to the court with additional stress for the child and other parties. The emphasis should be on ensuring the child is afforded *reasonable contact*[33] insofar as it promotes and does not prejudice his *welfare*[34].

---

29   CA 1989 s 1(3)(a)-(g).
30   CA 1989 s 1(3)(a)-(f).
31   CA 1989 s 34(11)(a); see chapter 9 – Contact order.
32   CA 1989 s 34(11)(b).
33   CA 1989 s 34(1).
34   CA 1989 Sch 2, para 15(1).

Options available to the court

The guardian ad litem is required to advise the court about the *options available to it in respect of the child, and the suitability of each option including what order should be made in determining the application*[35]. An examination of the criteria will be required for each of the options available to the court.

Where there are real conflicts of facts that only the court can resolve, the guardian ad litem's assessment should consider the alternatives that might arise, depending on the judge's or magistrates' finding of fact[36].

The guardian ad litem should make clear in her report the various options that are legally possible with regard to the disposal of the case and differentiate between her recommendation(s) and the options that are available to the court.

The guardian ad litem should consider whether orders other than those applied for should be made, bearing in mind the court's power to make orders of its own motion; this includes any order under section 8 and a family assistance order[37]. Consideration should be given to whether the court should exercise its powers under section 91(14) to restrict an applicant's right to make future applications without the leave of the court.

If the recommendations of the guardian ad litem are significantly different from those of the local authority, a full explanation should be provided and advice given to the court as to what other order(s) (if any) the court might make to secure the result advised by the guardian ad litem. In particular, guardians ad litem should remember that the court has no power to attach conditions to a final care order[38], save by way of contact.

Consideration should be given to the 'no order' principle[39], and whether an order is necessary to promote the child's interests and welfare. The guardian ad litem must explain why the child would be better off if the recommended order were made.

Recommendation

The recommendation should be stated clearly, outlining each order that is believed to be in the child's best interests.

In certain cases a guardian ad litem may have difficulty in formulating a view until the court has resolved certain issues of fact, which may only be capable of reliable determination when competing experts and other factual witnesses have given evidence and been cross-examined. If the guardian ad litem finds herself in such a situation it may be appropriate for

---

[35]   FPC (CA 1989) R 1991, r 11(4)(e) and FPR 1991, r 4.11(4)(e).
[36]   B v B (Procedure: Alleged Sexual Abuse) [1994] 1 FCR 809.
[37]   CA 1989 s 16.
[38]   Re T (A Minor) (Care Order: Conditions) [1994] 2 FLR 423.
[39]   CA 1989 s 1(5).

her to offer alternative recommendations, depending on the court's finding of fact[40].

This section should be followed by the guardian ad litem's signature and the date.

Summary

The structure of the report will necessarily vary according to the nature and type of each case and application. The main purpose of the report is to present information fully, coherently and clearly so that the court can make its judgment in full possession of the available facts and opinions. Regardless of the structure used the guardian ad litem should always consider:

- the wishes and feelings of the child (under a separate heading);
- the welfare check-list;
- the local authority's care plan;
- contact (under a separate heading);
- the options available to the court and whether an order is necessary to promote the child's interests and welfare (including the principle of 'no order').

---

40   B v B (Procedure: Alleged Sexual Abuse) [1994] 1 FCR 809.

PART 3

THE GUARDIAN AD LITEM AND THE COURT PROCESS

CHAPTER 5
COURT STRUCTURE

Introduction

The criminal and civil courts are inter-related and partly serviced by the same legal personnel. Figure one at the end of this chapter summarises the court structure in diagrammatic form.

Magistrates' court

Magistrates' courts are the lowest tier of courts and have both criminal and civil jurisdiction.

There are three types of magistrates courts:

- magistrates' courts dealing with adult non-family proceedings;
- youth courts dealing with criminal matters involving children from the ages of 10 to 17 (inclusive) and ultimately to 21 when the provisions of the Criminal Justice Act 1991 are fully implemented;
- family proceedings courts which deal with all applications made to it under the Children Act 1989, family matters generally and adoption.

Magistrates

Generally lay magistrates are not legally qualified. They are appointed by the Lord Chancellor, and are advised on the law by legally qualified justices' clerks. Magistrates who sit in the youth courts and family proceedings courts have to undergo certain additional training to equip them for these tasks.

Lay magistrates sit as a Bench comprising two or three magistrates of whom one acts as the chairperson and speaks on behalf of the court. In the family proceedings court the Bench must include both a man and a woman. A magistrate has limited powers when he sits alone; in relation to family proceedings he may make only emergency protection orders and recovery orders.

Stipendiary magistrates are legally qualified. They receive a salary and they usually sit alone.

Family Proceedings Court

This court deals initially with most, but not all, applications for care orders, supervision orders, other specified proceedings under the Children Act

1989 and adoption applications. It has the power to transfer more complicated cases to the county court and to consolidate where necessary.

The Crown Court

The Crown Court deals exclusively with criminal proceedings and cases are heard before a High Court judge, a circuit judge or a recorder. An appeal from the youth court and magistrates court (in criminal proceedings) is heard by a circuit judge with two lay magistrates by way of re-hearing the case.

The County Court

Care Centre

County courts designated as care centres may hear all applications under the Children Act 1989. Nominated circuit judges hear public law applications transferred from the family proceedings court or the High Court.

District judges at care centres may make directions in public and private law cases and deal with transfer applications refused by the family proceedings court that are referred for reconsideration. District judges have powers to make certain preliminary or limited and agreed orders in public and private law cases.

Care centres are also family hearing centres and divorce centres.

Principal Registry

In London the Principal Registry of the Family Division is the care centre.

Circuit judges sit at the Royal Courts of Justice to hear matters referred to them by district judges. Nominated district judges have powers more akin to a circuit judge.

Family hearing centres

County courts designated as family hearing centres are able to deal with applications under Part I, II and Schedule I of the Children Act 1989. Family hearing centres are not able to hear public law applications. Family hearing centres are also divorce centres.

Divorce centres

County courts designated as divorce centres may hear applications under Parts I, II and Schedule I of the Children Act 1989 with the exception of contested section 8 applications which must be transferred to a family hearing centre.

The High Court

The High Court has three divisions: Family Division, Chancery Division and Queen's Bench Division. High Court judges sit alone when adjudicating upon a case. District Registries located throughout the country can deal with High Court matters. District judges hear preliminary and interlocutory matters relating to these proceedings. The High Court also deals with appeals from the family proceedings court.

The Court of Appeal

The Court of Appeal has two divisions: criminal and civil. The Master of the Rolls is the Head of the Court of Appeal (Civil Division). Appeals are heard by two or three appeal judges sitting together. The Civil Division hears appeals from the High Court and county court.

The House of Lords

The House of Lords hears appeals from the Court of Appeal. Senior members of the judiciary have been made life peers (Law Lords) to enable them to sit as members of the Judicial Committee of the Upper House of Parliament.

How to address members of the Judiciary

- *Judges in the Court of Appeal*
  Judges are addressed in court as My Lord/Lady and collectively as My Lords; and referred to in reports as Lord Justice/Lady Justice X.

- *High Court Judges*
  Judges are addressed in court as My Lord/Lady; and referred to in reports as Mr/Mrs Justice X.

- *Circuit Judges*
  Judges are addressed in court as Your Honour; and referred to in reports as His/Her Honour Judge X.

- *District Judges*
  District Judges are addressed in court as Sir/Madam; and referred to in reports as District Judge X.

- *Magistrates*
  Magistrates are addressed in court as Sir/Madam and collectively as Your Worships; and referred to in reports as the Bench.

Correspondence to the court

- *High Court and the Principal Registry*
  Letters should be addressed to The Chief Clerk, Principal Registry of the Family Division.

- *County Court*
  Letters should be addressed to The Chief Clerk.

- *Magistrates Court*
  Letters should be addressed to The Clerk to the Justices and in Inner London to the Senior Chief Clerk.

FIGURE ONE: COURT STRUCTURE FOR PROCEEDINGS UNDER THE CHILDREN ACT 1989

HOUSE OF LORDS

- Appeals from Court of Appeal

COURT OF APPEAL (Civil Division)

- Appeals from High Court and county court

HIGH COURT (Family Division)

- Public and private law cases involving complex points or issues of law
- Private law applications made by children
- Applications when there are pending proceedings, or to vary, extend or discharge existing orders of the court.
- Appeals under CA 1989 from family proceedings court
- Inherent jurisdiction

COUNTY COURT

Care Centre

Circuit Judge

- Transferred public law cases
- Applications when there are pending proceedings, or to vary, extend or discharge existing orders of the court
- Private law cases

District Judge

- Directions in public and private law cases
- Transfer applications refused by family proceedings court referred for reconsideration
- Powers to make certain preliminary or limited and agreed orders in public and private law cases

Family Hearing Centre

Circuit Judge

- Private law cases

District Judge

- Directions in private law cases
- Powers to make preliminary and agreed orders in private law cases

---

FAMILY PROCEEDINGS COURT

- Most public law cases are commenced here
- Private law cases may be commenced here

CHAPTER 6
LEGAL REPRESENTATION

Introduction

The legal profession in England and Wales has two branches: barristers and solicitors. Despite the fact that solicitors and barristers do have different roles there is a great deal of overlap between the two professions. Solicitors have direct contact with their clients and, as well as representing their clients in court, may prepare the case for a barrister to represent the client in court. Barristers, on the other hand, usually act only as advocates and give opinions to solicitors on matters of law and practice. Both branches of the legal profession can be involved in specified proceedings under the Children Act 1989.

Solicitor

A solicitor may be a sole practitioner, a member of a partnership, or an employed assistant solicitor. Solicitors have clients with many different legal problems. They may, therefore, have to be generalists, although many will have specialist knowledge in certain areas. There are also some solicitors who choose to practise only in one particular area of the law.

Solicitors may act as advocates in child care proceedings in the family proceedings court, county courts, and in the High Court in most child care cases, as these proceedings will be heard in chambers. There will be no restriction upon the solicitor acting as the advocate throughout the child care case. If, however, a case (such as an appeal) is heard in open court in the Family Division of the High Court, a solicitor normally will not have right of audience.

Appointment of solicitor

The court may decide to appoint a solicitor where one has not already been appointed[1]. Before this can be done, however, one of the following conditions must be satisfied:

    (a) no guardian ad litem has been appointed for the child;
    (b) the child has sufficient understanding to instruct a solicitor and wishes to do so;

---

[1]   CA 1989 s 41(3).

> (c) it appears to the court that it would be in the child's best interests for him to be represented by a solicitor.
>
> *(CA 1989 s 41(4))*

A solicitor appointed under section 41(3) or in accordance with rule 11(2)(a) shall represent the child –

> (a) *in accordance with the instructions received from the guardian ad litem (unless the solicitor considers, having taken into account the views of the guardian ad litem and any direction of the court under rule 11(3), that the child wishes to give instructions which conflict with those of the guardian ad litem and that he is able, having regard to his understanding, to give such instructions on his own behalf in which case he shall conduct the proceedings in accordance with the instructions received from the child), or*
>
> (b) *where no guardian ad litem has been appointed for the child and the condition in section 41(4)(b) is satisfied, in accordance with instructions received from the child, or*
>
> (c) *in default of instructions under (a) or (b), in furtherance of the best interests of the child.*
>
> *(FPC (CA 1989) R 1991, r 12(1))*[2]

The child's solicitor will be appointed:

- by the court where no guardian ad litem has been appointed for the child;
- by the guardian ad litem where the child is too young to give instructions to the solicitor;
- by the guardian ad litem, court or the child, where a child is capable of giving him instructions. In the great majority of cases, the guardian ad litem will appoint the solicitor in the first instance, even if the child is capable of giving independent instruction to the solicitor.

If the solicitor is appointed by the court prior to the appointment of the guardian ad litem then the solicitor must:

- act in accordance with the child's instructions;
- act in the best interests of the child where the child is not capable of giving him instructions.

He should carry out the following tasks:

- make an application for legal aid;
- receive documentary evidence from the court;
- contact the local authority or the court to determine whether the child is actually in care;
- decide whether the child is capable of giving instructions;

---

2   FPR 1991, r 4.12(1).

- when attending any hearing, be sure the child is capable of giving instructions, if not, then act in the child's best interests;
- meet with the guardian ad litem when she is appointed to apprise her of developments.

Before the guardian ad litem decides to instruct a particular solicitor, he should check that the practitioner is a member of the Children Panel. Members of the Panel are solicitors who have been approved by the Law Society as practitioners with specialist knowledge in the area of child care law. It is not obligatory for a guardian ad litem to instruct a solicitor who is on the Children Panel.

Child instructing his solicitor

If the child is capable and competent to give instructions to the solicitor and the child's instructions conflict with those of the guardian ad litem, the solicitor must conduct the case under the instruction of the child. It is the task of the solicitor to ascertain whether or not the child is competent to give instructions; the solicitor will take into account the views of the guardian ad litem and any other experts involved in the proceedings.

The child's solicitor will consider the following guidance issued by the Solicitors Family Law Association[3] when assessing the child's understanding:

> "From the onset the solicitor will need to assess the child's understanding and capacity to give instructions. Maturity can be assessed on the child's ability to understand the nature of the proceedings and to have an appreciation of the possible consequences both in the long and short term of the applications to the court.
>
> The duty to assess a child's understanding is the solicitor's duty and it continues throughout the case. . . .
>
> If a solicitor is acting on the direct instructions of a child in specified proceedings, he cannot then represent the guardian before the court if there is a conflict between them. If he is in doubt as to the child's capacity to give instructions, and what the child is saying is in conflict with the guardian, the solicitor should seek the advice of one of the other professionals involved in the case such as a child psychiatrist, social worker or teacher, or an independent expert may have to be approached (for example, a child psychiatrist). When making these consultations the solicitor should remain sensitive to their duty of confidentiality to the child. Ultimately, an application can be made to the court.

3   Guide to Good Practice for Solicitors Acting for Children, Solicitors Family Law Association, 1994.

If it appears that a child's decision-making ability has become impaired, the solicitor should re-assess the child's capacity and consult with the guardian ad litem . . . "

The final decision as to whether the child is capable of instructing his solicitor rests with the court[4]. The guardian ad litem will be expected to advise the court[4] and make any representations she feels appropriate.

Where a child instructs his solicitor the following guidance[5] is provided regarding disclosure of and access to documents in the case:

"Under the professional rules solicitors are generally under a duty to allow clients unfettered access to any relevant documentary evidence which the solicitor holds, save where such evidence would adversely affect the client's physical or mental condition. However, as a matter of good practice, there may be exceptional cases such as serious child sexual abuse when the nature of the document is such that it would be inappropriate for clients to be sent a copy of the documentation for their retention. When representing a child, solicitors should be particularly careful about showing documents to the child and, if in any doubt as to whether a document should be disclosed, should seek the opinion of the guardian ad litem (if any) or any other professional involved in the case."

Where the guardian ad litem is concerned about the effect upon the child of the disclosure of certain documents to him, she should discuss the matter with the child's solicitor and advise the court[6].

Guardian ad litem instructing the child's solicitor

The guardian ad litem will be responsible for appointing and instructing the child's solicitor in specified proceedings[7], except where the child is of sufficient understanding (see above).

The role of the solicitor is to act as the legal adviser to the guardian ad litem and to represent the child, by taking instructions from the guardian ad litem. Even where the child is not old enough to give instructions to the solicitor, it is often appropriate for the solicitor to meet the child whom he is representing. Such a meeting will usually take place in the presence of the guardian ad litem.

All members of the Law Society's Children Panel give an undertaking to conduct the case for the child personally and not to delegate it to another solicitor or counsel unless it is unavoidable or the solicitor considers it in the best interests of the child.

---

4   Re M (Minors) (Care Proceedings: Child's Wishes) [1994] 1 FLR 749.
5   Guide to Good Practice for Solicitors Acting for Children, Solicitors Family Law Association, 1994.
6   FPC (CA 1989) R 1991 r 11(4)(f) and FPR 1991 r 4.11(4)(f).
7   FPC (CA 1989) R 1991, r 11(2)(a) and FPR 1991, r 4.11(2)(a); see chapter 3 – Powers and duties of the guardian ad litem.

Tasks and issues that need to be discussed and covered by the solicitor and guardian ad litem together in the course of the case are as follows:

- arrange for the solicitor to meet the child;
- allocate tasks;
- examine the evidence;
- decide whether experts are to be instructed and, if so, the arrangements for funding (i.e. legal aid in most cases);
- examine the law;
- decide whether to instruct counsel;
- consider transfer.

In order to avoid duplication, there should be regular dialogue and communication between the solicitor and guardian ad litem throughout the case, whether this be at court, before or after hearings, in meetings at the solicitor's office or on the telephone.

One of the main tasks of the solicitor is to advise the guardian ad litem on the law. It is the function of the solicitor to make the guardian ad litem aware of the various orders at the court's disposal, their possible combinations and the relevant law generally.

Counsel may be instructed to attend directions hearings where the solicitor for the child is unavailable. Equally, in such circumstances, the solicitor for the child could decide, in consultation with the guardian ad litem, to instruct another solicitor to attend the directions hearing acting on an agency basis. Where it has been decided that counsel is to conduct the final hearing, it is often useful to have counsel attending a final directions hearing if issues in dispute are to be determined.

Instruction of barrister (counsel)

Barristers are principally advocates who conduct cases in court. They may also give "opinions" on legal problems. The Bar does not have a specialist "Children Panel". A barrister will not normally deal with a client direct, but must be briefed by a solicitor. If it is decided to instruct counsel, it is still necessary for the guardian ad litem to instruct a solicitor who, in turn, instructs counsel.

Unless the child is old enough to instruct the solicitor separately, the guardian ad litem should be consulted by the solicitor about the choice of counsel to be instructed. The guardian ad litem should be willing to take the initiative in discussing the use of counsel.

The barrister may meet the child where the child is giving direct instructions to the solicitor. It may be appropriate to have a conference with the child prior to the hearing if the child is of sufficient age and understanding.

Applications to terminate the appointment of the solicitor

The child may apply to the court to terminate the appointment of the solicitor[8]. The solicitor and guardian ad litem must be given the opportunity to express an opinion upon this matter.

The guardian ad litem may also apply to have the appointment of the solicitor terminated[9]. The solicitor, and the child if of sufficient understanding, must be given the opportunity to voice an opinion. On any such application, the court must give reasons for its decision to remove a solicitor[10].

There may be a variety of reasons why a guardian ad litem may want to terminate the appointment of a solicitor. For example:

■ the solicitor may be refusing to take instructions from the guardian ad litem;
■ the solicitor may not be able to communicate with the child;
■ the guardian ad litem may lack confidence in the solicitor's capabilities;
■ the breakdown in the professional relationship between the guardian ad litem and the solicitor;
■ it may be desirable for the same solicitor to represent another child of the family in the same proceedings.

Funding legal representation

Legal aid[11] is usually available in specified proceedings, though not to a local authority or a guardian ad litem acting alone.

Where the guardian ad litem separates from the child's solicitor she may, with leave of the court, appoint a solicitor to act for her in the proceedings. Legal aid is not available to finance such legal representation. The guardian ad litem must negotiate with her Panel manager to arrange for the local authority to pay for any legal expenses incurred. It is not a good idea for a guardian ad litem to attempt to carry out an advocacy role herself. Guardians ad litem are not advocates and it is therefore appropriate to engage a legal representative at the earliest possible opportunity, with leave of the court[12]. The guidance issued by the Department of Health[13] and the Regulations[14] indicate that local authorities should be prepared to pay the guardian ad litem's reasonable legal costs in such cases.

---

8   FPC (CA 1989) R 1991, r 12(3) and FPR 1991 r 4.12(3).
9   FPC (CA 1989) R 1991, r 12(4) and FPR 1991 r 4.12(4).
10   FPC (CA 1989) R 1991, r 12(5) and FPR 1991 r 4.12(5).
11   The Legal Aid Act 1988.
12   FPC (CA 1989) R 1991 r 11(3) and FPR 1991 r 4.11(3).
13   CA 1989 Guidance and Regulations vol 7: Guardians ad Litem and other Court Related issues, para 2.36, p 9.
14   Guardian ad Litem and Reporting Officer (Panels) Regulations 1991 (SI 1991/2051) reg 9(1).

Giving advice to parties with regard to the selection of a solicitor

If a guardian ad litem is asked by parents for the names of solicitors to give them legal advice the guardian ad litem should be very careful not to influence the selection. The guardian ad litem should give not less than three practitioners' names from the Children Panel, as well as informing the parents that they may use their own solicitor if they have one, or seek further advice from their local citizen's advice bureau, thereby ensuring a choice from which to make a selection. Some courts provide lists of local solicitors who are members of the Children Panel.

Summary

The relationship between the guardian ad litem and solicitor should be one of partnership and mutual professional respect. Although the roles of the guardian ad litem and the solicitor are different there is some overlap. Where the child is not able to instruct his solicitor the guardian ad litem will, on his behalf, determine the instructions given to the child's solicitor. The guardian ad litem should be guided by the advice of the child's solicitor regarding the law and its application to the case.

CHAPTER 7
EXPERT REPORTS

Introduction

No person may, without leave of the justices' clerk or the court, cause the child to be medically or psychiatrically examined, or otherwise assessed, for the purpose of the preparation of expert evidence for use in the proceedings.

(FPC (CA 1989) R 1991 r 18(1))[1]

At an early stage the guardian ad litem will need to consider whether any expert reports and assessments are required in order to assist the court in its consideration of the case. An agreement between parties about the expert or experts to be used may help reduce any areas of conflict, and therefore the length of the final hearing. No child may be seen by an expert for the purposes of preparing a report for the proceedings without leave of the court[1].

From the child's point of view it is likely to be better to avoid repeat assessments and interviews by different experts. The guardian ad litem should make representations to the court at a directions hearing if she feels that the child's welfare is being or is likely to be prejudiced in this way.

Medical or psychiatric examinations or other assessments

"Where the court makes an interim care order, or interim supervision order, it may give such directions (if any) as it considers appropriate with regard to the medical or psychiatric examination or other assessment of the child; but if the child is of sufficient understanding to make an informed decision he may refuse to submit to the examination or other assessment."

(CA 1989 s 38(6))

When making an interim order, the court may direct that there be no such examination or assessment, or that there be none unless the court directs otherwise[2]. The court may direct that a medical or psychiatric examination takes place at any time while the interim order is still in force. The court can direct that a local authority carries out such a medical or psychiatric examination or other assessment, even where the local authority is opposed to that course of action[3].

---

1   FPR 1991 r 4.18(1).
2   CA 1989 s 38(7).
3   Re O (Minors) (Medical Examination) [1993] 1 FLR 860.

The range of medical or psychiatric examinations or other assessments necessary for the case will vary according to the nature of the case and to the questions needing to be answered. The court will look to the guardian ad litem for advice about:

> *whether the child is of sufficient understanding for any purpose including the child's refusal to submit to the medical or psychiatric examination or other assessment that the court has the power to require, direct or order;*
>
> *(FPC (CA 1989) R 1991, r 11(4)(a))*[4]

When considering the choice of expert to be consulted the guardian ad litem should take account, as appropriate, of the child's race, religion, language, gender and any special needs.

The type of examinations or assessments which might be ordered are as follows:

- psychiatric assessment of the child with or without the presence of the parents;
- psychiatric assessment of the family functioning and relationships between relevant adults and/or the child;
- assessment of contact between a child and a parent or other significant adult;
- paediatric review of the child, including examination;
- paediatric examination of child regarding symptoms of abuse at issue in the court proceedings;
- developmental assessment of child, usually carried out by a community medical officer and/or psychologist;
- specific assessments regarding a child's communication skills or ability to comprehend matters being discussed; these might be carried out by speech and language therapist, or an expert in communicating with hearing impaired children or in communicating with children with learning difficulties;
- expert assessments of any other matter in issue in the proceedings.

A psychiatric assessment may involve a team of professionals led by a child psychiatrist and include assessments by a child psychotherapist, clinical psychologist, social worker, and child psychiatric nurse.

In certain circumstances, it may only be necessary for papers and reports to be sent to a particular expert for an opinion, subject to leave being obtained from the court. Courts have been directed not to make generalised orders giving leave for the papers to be shown to 'an expert' or 'experts'[5]. In each case, the expert or area of expertise should be identified. There is an obligation upon the parties to disclose any report to all the parties whether or not the report is favourable to that party.

---

4   FPC (CA 1989) R 1991, r 11(4)(a) and FPR 1991, r 4.11(4)(a); see chapter 9 – Direction appointments and hearings.

5   Re G (Minors) (Expert Witnesses) [1994] 2 FLR 291.

The list of factors that the court should take into account when considering whether or not to give permission for a particular expert to undertake a particular examination or assessment are[6]:

- the category of expert evidence which the party in question seeks to adduce;
- the relevance of the expert evidence to the issues arising for decision in the case;
- whether or not the expert evidence can be properly obtained by the joint instruction of one expert by two or more parties;
- whether expert evidence in any given category may properly be adduced by only one party (for example, by the guardian ad litem) or whether it is necessary for experts in the same discipline to be instructed by more than one party.

Choice of expert

The choice of expert will depend on the nature of the assessment, the level of expertise required and the timetable for the proceedings.

Depending on the issues in the case it may be essential to ensure that an expert who is acknowledged to be an authority in a particular field is engaged. Such experts may not be able to complete the required assessment within the court's timetable.

Consideration should be given as to whether an expert with general knowledge in a particular field rather than an authority would be adequate for the case.

The issue of the level of expertise required and any possible consequent delay should be considered at a directions appointment. The guardian ad litem will need to balance the provision of suitable expertise for the child's case with the implications of any delay and make representations accordingly. Judges are generally well aware of, and reasonably sympathetic to, the shortage of suitable experts and the consequent pressure on their diaries.

Consulting the parties

Department of Health guidance[7] indicates that the guardian ad litem is expected to ascertain the child's views and the position of the parties regarding any assessments to be carried out. Where there is conflict between the parties, the court is expected to determine the type of assessment to be carried out, and by whom, based on the nature of the concern and what is in the best interests of the child.

---

6   Re G (Minors) (Expert Witness) [1994] 2 FLR 291.
7   CA 1989 Guidance and Regulations vol 1: Court Orders, para 3.49 p 31.

Consent of the child

Having identified the sorts of assessment or examination required, the guardian ad litem is required to consult with the child about the proposed examination or assessment, subject to the child's age and understanding. If the child is of sufficient understanding to make an informed decision to refuse to submit to an examination, the court in specified proceedings does not have the power to over-ride the child's refusal. A child of sixteen is presumed in law to be capable of giving, or withholding, consent unless there is some mental incapacity to the giving of consent.

In the face of the child's refusal to consent to an examination or assessment, the guardian ad litem will be required to explain the child's reasoning, and to give consideration to the merits of the likely evidential value of any assessment that is carried out against the child's wishes. In such circumstances it may be appropriate to consider sending such reports that are available to a relevant expert for an opinion, insofar as one can be offered without an examination or assessment, regarding the matters to be considered[8].

Where a child refuses to consent, the High Court, in the exercise of its inherent jurisdiction[9], has the power to override the child's refusal if it is in his best interests to do so. Notwithstanding the court overriding the child's wishes the responsible clinician must make a clinical judgment at the time of the assessment or examination as to whether to proceed.

Instructing an expert

The letter of instruction to the expert should be written by the solicitor commissioning him and should indicate whether there is agreement between the parties about both the expert's appointment and the instructions given.

Where the expert has been appointed on behalf of the child, the child's solicitor will write the letter of instruction based upon the instructions of the guardian ad litem. It must clearly set out the context in which the expert's opinion is sought and define carefully the specific questions the expert is being asked to address[10]. The letter of instruction should list the documents which are sent to the expert. The letter of instruction will be required by the court, together with the expert's report[10]. This letter becomes part of the documentation in the case[10].

It is good practice for the guardian ad litem, through the child's solicitor, to canvass the other parties for any specific areas they wish the expert to investigate before finalising the letter of instruction.

The guardian ad litem should aim to ensure that any experts instructed on behalf of the child are kept up to date with new developments in the case[10],

---

8   See chapter 9 – Directions appointments and hearings.
9   Re E (A Minor) (Wardship: Medical Treatment) [1993] 1 FLR 382.
10   Re M (Minors) (Care Proceedings: Child's Wishes) [1994] 1 FLR 749.

so that they are fully apprised of matters prior to giving evidence in any final hearing.

Where there are significant differences of opinion between experts, the guardian ad litem and child's solicitor together with other advocates should always consider asking the experts to discuss matters with one another prior to a final hearing to narrow the areas of disagreement[11] that are relevant for the court when considering the application. It may be appropriate for the experts as well as discussing areas of agreement and disagreement to set out in writing their concluding position. If the guardian ad litem feels that this course of action would assist the court, she should seek a direction from the court to this effect[12]. The guardian ad litem and the child's solicitor may need to consider in certain cases whether to prepare a written schedule clarifying the areas of agreement and disagreement between the experts[13].

Role and duties of an expert

With regard to the duties and role of the expert, it has been stated[14]:

> "Expert witnesses are in a privileged position; indeed, only experts are permitted to give an opinion in evidence. Outside the legal field the court itself has no expertise and for that reason frequently has to rely on the evidence of experts. Such experts must express only opinions which they genuinely hold and which are not biased in favour of one particular party. Opinions can, of course, differ and indeed quite frequently experts who have expressed their objective and honest opinions will differ, but such differences are usually within the legitimate area of disagreement. On occasion, and because they are acting on opposing sides, each may give his opinion from a different basic fact. This of itself is likely to produce a divergence."

Further points to consider with regard to expert opinion[14] are that:

- the expert should not mislead by omissions. He should consider all the material facts in reaching his conclusions and must not omit to consider the material facts which could detract from his concluded opinion;
- if experts look for a report on facts which tend to support a particular proposition or case, their reports should still:
  - provide a straightforward, not a misleading opinion;
  - be objective and not omit factors which do not support their opinion; and
  - be properly researched;

---

11   Re M (Minors) (Care Proceedings: Child's Wishes) [1994] 1 FLR 749.
12   Re G (Minors) (Expert Witnesses) [1994] 2 FLR 291.
13   Re C (Expert Evidence: Disclosure: Practice) [1995] 1 FLR 204.
14   Re R (A Minor) (Expert's Evidence) (Note) [1991] 1 FLR 291.

- if the expert's opinion is not properly researched because he considers that insufficient data is available, he must say so and indicate that his opinion is no more than a provisional one;
- in certain circumstances an expert may find that he has to give an opinion adverse to his client. Alternatively, if, contrary to the appropriate practice, an expert does provide a report which is other than wholly objective – that is one which seeks to promote a particular case – the report should make this clear. However, such an approach should be avoided because it would:
  - be an abuse of the position of an expert's function and privilege; and
  - render the report an argument and not an opinion;
- a misleading opinion from an expert may well inhibit a proper assessment of a particular case by the non-medical professional advisers and may also lead parties, and in particular parents, to false views and hopes;
- misleading expert opinion is likely to increase costs by requiring competing evidence to be called at the hearing on issues which should in fact be non-contentious;
- the duty to be objective and not to mislead is as vital as in any case because the child's welfare, which is a matter of extreme importance, is at stake, and his interests are paramount. An absence of objectivity may result in a child being wrongly placed and thereby unnecessarily put at risk;
- in all cases there is likely to be a reduction in the scale of scientific issues and a consequential saving in costs, if arrangements are made for the experts on each side to discuss together their reports in advance of the hearing.

Summary

In considering her advice to the court, the guardian ad litem should be mindful of her duty to promote and safeguard the welfare of the child, and the need to avoid delay unless it can be shown to be purposeful[15]. The guardian ad litem may be able to suggest an expert acceptable to all parties. A proliferation of experts in a case will cause delay and will lengthen the time estimate for any hearing. The court will look to the guardian ad litem for advice as to whether the child is likely to suffer significantly adverse effects as a result of being subjected to further interviews or medical examination.

---

15   CA 1989 s 1(2).

CHAPTER 8
EVIDENCE

Introduction

This chapter is a brief introduction to the subject of evidence, and does not set out to be comprehensive. This chapter introduces the subject and lists the types of evidence commonly found in children's cases. Any problems that the guardian ad litem encounters with regard to evidence should be discussed with the solicitor for the child.

Rules of evidence

Some rules of evidence are in statutory form; others are found in the common law. With regard to children cases, the common law rules of evidence apply, but specific exceptions under the Children Act 1989[1], subsequent regulations[2] and the inherent jurisdiction of the High Court mean that the strict exclusionary rules of evidence are modified in this area of the law.

Specific exceptions under the Children Act 1989

The Children Act 1989 provides for the following exceptions to the law of evidence:

- the court may take account of any information included in the guardian ad litem's report as long as it is relevant and any evidence given in respect of matters referred to in the report[3];
- the court may take account of information contained in records held by the local authority and copied by the guardian ad litem[4] in respect of any matters referred to in the guardian ad litem's report or evidence[5];
- in an application for an emergency protection order, the court may take account of any relevant statements in a report made in connection with the hearing or any relevant evidence, notwithstanding any rule of law or enactment which would render it otherwise inadmissible[6].

---

1   CA 1989 s 45(7).
2   Children (Admissibility of Hearsay Evidence) Order 1993 and CA 1989 45(7) Courts & Legal Services Act 1990.
3   CA 1989 s 41(11).
4   CA 1989 s 42.
5   CA 1989 s 42(2).
6   CA 1989 s 45(7).

Types of evidence

There are basically four types of evidence: documentary, oral, real and expert. All evidence has to be relevant to the issues before the court.

Documentary evidence

There is provision in the Rules for two types of documentary evidence[7];

- statement of the substance of oral evidence to be given;
- documents plus expert reports. Documentary evidence may include video and audio tape recordings, local authority records and health records.

Oral evidence

Usually it is necessary for a court to hear oral evidence before adjudicating on a child care case. In practice courts do not always demand oral evidence at every stage of the proceedings. It may suffice that a written statement is presented and the author of that statement is available for cross examination. Oral evidence by a witness who has not filed a statement can only be given with the leave of the court.

Real evidence

This is a category of evidence that has limited relevance to children's proceedings. It usually takes the form of an object produced for inspection to the court in order that the court may draw some inference or make observations about it. Examples of real evidence in child care cases would include:

- children's drawings;
- x-rays of any injury;
- photographs;
- video recordings.

Although real evidence in proceedings is valuable in terms of proof, it is of little value per se. In addition to physical objects, real evidence includes the physical appearance of persons, the demeanour of witnesses and, more importantly, in child care cases, the intonation of voices on video or tape recordings and body language.

Expert evidence[8]

Leave of the court is necessary for a child to be examined, by an expert, for the purpose of preparing a report for the proceedings[9]. This includes

---

7   FPC (CA 1989) R 1991, r 17 and FPR 1991, r 4.17.
8   See chapter 7 – Expert reports.
9   FPC (CA 1989) R 1991, r 18(1) and FPR 1991 r 4.18(1).

psychiatric or psychological assessment and any other non-physical examination. Leave is also necessary to disclose court papers to experts.

Giving evidence

Initially witnesses give their evidence by replying aloud to questions from their own legal representative; this is called 'examination in chief'. Sometimes the witnesses' written statements or reports may be taken to be "evidence in chief" without further elaboration. The legal representatives for other parties, or the parties themselves if not represented by a lawyer, may cross-examine the witnesses on matters in dispute or other matters not led in chief and the court may wish to ask questions for clarification. The legal representatives may call the witness to be 're-examined' for clarification but not to introduce new evidence.

All witnesses commence their evidence by giving their name, address, occupation, qualifications, and experience (if a professional witness). A guardian ad litem should not give her personal address but the address of the panel of guardians ad litem and reporting officers or that of the court.

When a witness gives his evidence he should address his answers to the judge or the bench. Even where the court has the facility for tape recording the evidence, the judge or magistrates may wish to take their own notes. Therefore the witness should give his evidence at such a speed as to facilitate the taking of notes. When a guardian ad litem wishes to refer to her own file and notes she should ask the court's permission. If the guardian ad litem is allowed to refer to her notes the advocates will be entitled to inspect those notes. If the guardian ad litem is cross-examined on the notes, the notes themselves become part of the evidence admitted in the proceedings. The guardian ad litem should keep her whole file with her whilst giving evidence and should feel free to refer to any document providing she identifies the document.

Evidence in proceedings under the Children Act 1989

An application is commenced by completing the appropriate form and lodging it with the court. A copy of the form is also served on the other parties to the case. Notice of the proceedings must also be served on other persons specified in the rules. In public law proceedings directions will be given requiring the parties to file their written evidence in accordance with the court's timetable. This enables each party to be aware of facts or allegations made and to identify each party's position.

At the hearing the parties will give evidence in the following order, subject to specific directions being given by the court[10]:

---

10   FPC (CA 1989) R 1991, r 21(2)(3) and FPR 4.21(2)(3).

- applicants;
- parties with parental responsibility;
- any other respondents;
- guardian ad litem if appointed;
- the child when no guardian ad litem has been appointed.

The rules do not provide for the situation where a child gives separate instructions from the guardian ad litem. In such circumstances the court would determine the order of evidence most appropriate to the situation. Usually the guardian ad litem will be last.

The standard of proof

In criminal proceedings the standard of proof required before an alleged offence is proved is that an offence must be proved beyond reasonable doubt. In civil proceedings facts must be proved on the balance of probabilities. It is to this standard that facts which are said have caused or amounted to significant harm must be proved. In cases of serious allegations (such as the those of sexual abuse) it has been said frequently by the Court of Appeal that the facts must be proven to a high standard of probability, commensurate with the gravity of the allegation. In practice this means that the court must look searchingly at the evidence, and will be reluctant to find that sexual abuse has been perpetrated (especially by a named individual) unless the evidence is clear and cogent. The graver the allegations, the more cogent must be the proof[11].

Whether the child has suffered significant harm is again a question of fact, to be decided on the balance of probabilities. However, where it is contended that the child is likely to suffer significant harm in the future, it is sufficient that the court finds, on the basis of its findings of fact as to the past events, that a significant risk of future significant harm exists.

Sir Stephen Brown, President of the Family Division, stated in a Court of Appeal decision[12]:

> "I very much hope that in approaching cases under the Children Act 1989 courts will not be invited to perform in every case a strict legalistic analysis of the statutory meaning of section 31. Of course, the words of the statute must be considered, but I do not believe that Parliament intended them to be unduly restrictive when the evidence clearly indicates that a certain course should be taken in order to protect the child."

The burden of proof

In any judicial proceedings it is for the party bringing the proceedings to satisfy the statutory criteria for the order being sought.

---

11   Re W (Minors) (Sexual Abuse: Standard of Proof) [1994] 1 FLR 419.
12   Newham London Borough Council v AG [1993] 1 FLR 281.

There are three distinct aspects of proving the case known as the burden of proof:

- adducing evidence which, if believed, will be sufficient for the necessary allegations to be proved is called the legal burden;
- the burden of proving to the court that the adduced evidence is admissible;
- the need to adduce evidence as to a particular fact, referred to as the evidential burden or the persuasive burden.

The legal burden stays with the party bringing the proceedings, whilst the evidential burden can shift to other parties depending upon how the case proceeds. In care proceedings, the legal burden will stay with the local authority i.e. they must prove the case by bringing sufficient credible evidence. Whether the court regards the evidence as sufficient will depend on its assessment of whether particular pieces of evidence should be accepted or rejected. This in turn will depend largely on how well the local authority's (and any supporting party's) evidence has stood up to cross examination, and the court's assessment of any evidence which has been produced in rebuttal. In care proceedings the local authority must prove its case with evidence that establishes the threshold criteria and the need for an order.

In an application to discharge a care order, the burden rests with the applicant, whether it is the parent, the child or the local authority. The applicants must satisfy the court that discharge of the order is in the best interests of the child. Where the parents apply for the discharge of a care order, they must present their case first because they are the applicants. This applies when a parent makes a section 34 application for contact in respect of a child in care.

Compellability and competence

In general, all witnesses can be compelled to give evidence subject to privilege, e.g. a solicitor cannot be compelled to give evidence about his client's instructions. Most witnesses are also deemed to be competent, with two exceptions:

- persons who are not mentally capable;
- children.

When a child is giving evidence, the court must ascertain whether he is competent.

> *The child's evidence may be heard by the court if, in its opinion –*
>
> a) *he understands that it is his duty to speak the truth; and*
> b) *he has sufficient understanding to justify his evidence being heard.*
>
> *(CA 1989 s 96(2))*

If the court determines that the child does not understand the oath, the child's unsworn evidence may be heard, but only if the court thinks that he understands the duty to tell the truth and has sufficient understanding to justify his evidence being heard[13]. After giving unsworn testimony, the child is still liable to cross examination.

In Children Act cases the court normally will be reluctant to receive a child's evidence directly, since it can be given by the guardian ad litem. The court will require carefully reasoned advice from the guardian ad litem as to why it should hear directly from the child.

If the court decides to accept unsworn evidence, the guardian ad litem should be ready to advise on the means by which the evidence shall be taken – in court, behind a screen, or through closed circuit television.

In proceedings under Parts IV and V of the Children Act 1989, no person shall be excused from giving evidence on the grounds of incriminating himself or his spouse[14]. Doctors can also be compelled to give evidence about relevant matters covered by medical privilege if ordered to do so by a court. Indeed, in general where the welfare of the child demands it, professional privilege may be over-ridden except between solicitor and client.

The guardian ad litem may have to consider whether to seek a witness summons in respect of a reluctant witness, although that is a course which should be embarked upon only after careful consideration. This may also apply to professional witnesses or experts who are unwilling, for whatever reason, to attend the court hearing without a witness summons.

Access to local authority records

The guardian ad litem has a statutory right to have access to local authority records regarding the child.

> *Where a person has been appointed as a guardian ad litem under this Act he shall have the right at all reasonable times to examine and take copies of –*
>
> a) *any records of, or held by, a local authority (or an authorised person) which were compiled in connection with the making, or proposed making, by any person of any application under this Act with respect to the child concerned;*
> b) *any records of, or held by, a local authority which were compiled in connection with any functions which stand referred to their social services committee under the Local Authority Social Services Act 1970, so far as those records relate to that child; or*

---

13   CA 1989 s 96(2).
14   CA 1989 s 98.

c) *any records of, or held by, an authorised person which were compiled in connection with the activities of that person, so far as those records relate to that child.*

(CA 1989 s 42(1))

Where a guardian ad litem takes a copy of any record which he is entitled to examine under this section, that copy or any part of it shall be admissible as evidence of any matter referred to in any –

a) *report which he makes to the court in the proceedings in question; or*
b) *evidence which he gives in those proceedings.*

(CA 1989 s 42(2))

The above subsection over-rides any other legislation or rule which could prevent admissibility. "Authorised person" means the same as in section 31[15].

The guardian ad litem may produce relevant local authority records relating to the child, i.e. social services and education department records, as part of the evidence on behalf of the child. Consideration must be given to whether such records should be produced to the court, because this will normally lead to them being produced to all parties to the proceedings[16].

Records held by local authorities in respect of the parents of the child or any other relative or significant other, are not covered by this section. Authority is required from the person concerned before the local authority can grant access to any such file. Where the guardian ad litem identifies documents which she believes to be relevant she should discuss the matter with the child's solicitor who may invite the local authority to disclose the documents. If the local authority oppose the disclosure of the documents citing 'public interest immunity' the guardian ad litem and the child's solicitor should raise the matter at a directions appointment[17].

Evidence in sexual abuse cases

Evidence of child sexual abuse may come from a number of sources such as:

- the child;
- the child's behaviour or demeanour;
- the child's account of events and interpretation of it;
- parents, relatives, friends of the family or other adults;
- experts, including medical and psychiatric evidence;
- physical examination, including photographs;
- admission by a perpetrator.

---

15 CA 1989 s 31(9); see chapter 17 – Care and supervision orders.
16 FRC (CA 1989) R 1991, r 11(9)(b) and FPR 1991 r 4.11(9)(b).
17 Re C (Expert Evidence: Disclosure: Practice) [1995] 1 FLR 204.

Where diagnostic interviews are to form part of an assessment for the proceedings, then leave for the interviews must be sought and granted by the court. Failure to do so may render the evidence inadmissible unless the court gives permission for its admission in any event.

Children who are suspected of having been sexually abused should, wherever practicable, be video taped when interviewed. If the allegation is disputed, then the parties may wish to see the video recording and a transcript before the hearing. The court may also wish to view the video recording before making any decision. When a child has been interviewed more than once, the court may attach less weight to interviews carried out subsequently, subject to expert advice. Interviews used in therapy will rarely be used in the court proceedings.

The following faults with regard to child interviews should be avoided[18]:

- use of untrained and inexperienced interviewers;
- failure to approach the interview with an open mind;
- use of leading questions;
- too many interviews with each child;
- interviews conducted at the pace of adults rather than children;
- use of inadequate video and audio recording;
- lack of background information for interviewers;
- use of too many interviewers, either together or in sequence;
- telling the child what another child has said;
- pressure and anxiety to obtain results.

Where an interview takes place with a child witness for the purposes of criminal proceedings, it is regulated by the Memorandum of Good Practice issued by the Department of Health and Home Office[19]. This document is solely for use in criminal proceedings, although its' advice and guidance may be used by civil courts when deciding the weight to be given to this type of evidence.

Summary

Whether the court can make an order will be determined by its consideration of the evidence it receives. The child's solicitor is responsible for considering the available evidence on behalf of the child. The guardian ad litem must look to the solicitor for advice about the value of the evidence and consider what enquiries she needs to undertake in order to advise the court fully.

---

18   Re A and Others (Minors) (Child Abuse Guidelines) [1992] 1 FLR 439.
19   HMSO 1992.

CHAPTER 9
DIRECTIONS APPOINTMENTS AND HEARINGS

Introduction

Directions appointments and hearings, (referred to as "directions hearings"), have two main purposes:

- to maintain the court's control and direction of a particular case;
- to deal with procedural issues which require attention to ensure the case is ready to be heard at the final hearing.

Directions hearings

Directions hearings are held in all tiers of the court structure in specified proceedings. The guardian ad litem can make use of directions hearings to help plan the preparation of the case and any assessments that might be required, and to influence the progress of the case in the child's interests.

Directions hearings are one of the means by which the court tries to avoid delay as required by section 1(2) which states:

> *In any proceedings in which any question with respect to the upbringing of a child arises, the court shall have regard to the general principle that any delay in determining the question is likely to prejudice the welfare of the child.*
>
> *(CA 1989 s 1(2))*

The court is required to draw up a timetable and ensure, so far as possible, that it is adhered to:

> *A court hearing an application for an order under this Part shall (in the light of any rules made by virtue of subsection (2)) –*
>
> *(a) draw up a timetable with a view to disposing of the application without delay; and*
>
> *(b) give such directions as it considers appropriate for the purpose of ensuring, so far as is reasonably practical, that that timetable is adhered to.*
>
> *Rules of court may –*
>
> *(a) specify periods within which specified steps must be taken in relation to such proceedings; and*
>
> *(b) make other provision with respect to such proceedings for the purpose of ensuring, so far as is reasonably practicable, that they are disposed of without delay.*
>
> *(CA 1989 s 32(1))*

Section 32 refers to all applications under Part IV of the Children Act. Applications under Part V (orders for emergency protection of children) and secure accommodation order proceedings[1] are excluded. The Rules which to date have been made are Family Proceedings Rules and Family Proceedings Court (Children Act 1989) Rules 1991. They are updated and amended, so attention must be paid to ensure the relevant rules are applied.

Court Rules specifically require the guardian ad litem to advise the court about the appropriate forum for the proceedings and the appropriate timing of the proceedings[2]. The guardian ad litem should also advise the court about any other matters about which either the court seeks the guardian ad litem's advice or the guardian ad litem feels the court should be informed[3].

The Rules relating to directions hearings specify the issues upon which the court might require advice from the guardian ad litem.

> *In proceedings to which this Part applies the court may, subject to para (3), give, vary or revoke directions for the conduct of the proceedings, including –*
>
> (a) *the timetable for the proceedings;*
> (b) *varying the time within which or by which an act is required, by these rules or by other rules of court, to be done;*
> (c) *the attendance of the child;*
> (d) *the appointment of a guardian ad litem, whether under section 41 or otherwise, or of a solicitor under section 41(3);*
> (e) *the service of documents;*
> (f) *the submission of evidence including experts' reports;*
> (g) *the preparation of welfare reports under section 7;*
> (h) *the transfer of the proceedings to another court;*
> (i) *consolidation with other proceedings.*
>
> *(FPC (CA 1989) R 1991 r 14(2))*[4]

Directions hearings take place in front of a district judge in the county court and High Court and in the family proceedings court before a justices' clerk. There may be circumstances where directions hearings are heard by magistrates, or a county or High Court judge, particularly if a decision is required about a contested application.

---

1   CA 1989 s 25.
2   FPC (CA 1989) R 1991, r 11 (4)(c)(d) and FPR 1991 r 4.11(4)(c)(d).
3   FPC (CA 1989) R 1991, r 11 (4)(f) and FPR 1991 r 4.11(4)(f).
4   FPR 1991 r 4.14(2).

Timetable for the proceedings

As soon as it is practical to do so, the guardian ad litem should recommend that a final hearing date is fixed by the court. When considering dates for the final hearing the guardian ad litem should check that the proposed date for the final hearing does not clash with any other hearing commitments the guardian ad litem may have.

The guardian ad litem must ensure that the case, in the child's interests, has been thoroughly explored and prepared prior to the final hearing. In the child's interest balance should be preserved between the need to avoid delay and the need to ensure that paramount consideration is given to the child's welfare and that all options are considered. In some situations this may mean the guardian ad litem has to recommend some constructive or planned delay in the disposal of the matter, for example where an assessment is required.

The guardian ad litem and the child's solicitor, because of their responsibility for promoting the child's interests, will be in the best position to advise the court about these matters.

Appropriate forum to hear the case

The rules regarding transfer of cases are to be found in the Children (Allocation of Proceedings) Order 1991[5]. This has been summarised in figure two. The Children Act Advisory Committee Annual Report 1992/93[6] stated:

"The order provides for: −

- lateral transfer between family proceedings courts and lateral transfers between county courts when, in both cases, that is deemed to be in the best interests of the child (having regard first to the principle of avoiding delay) because it will accelerate the determination of proceedings, or will enable the matter to be heard with other family proceedings, or for the some other reason;
- transfer from family proceedings court to county courts where such transfer is deemed to be in the best interests of the child (having regard first to the principle of avoiding delay) if the case is exceptionally grave, important or complex, or should be heard with other family proceedings, or to accelerate the determination of proceedings;
- transfer from the county court to the High Court if the county court considers the proceedings to be more suitable for hearing in the High Court (e.g. a precedent is to be set or a major principle involved) and that it is in the best interests of the child;
- transfer down from the High Court to a county court where this is appropriate for reasons of consolidation with other proceedings."

---

5   SI 1991/1677.
6   The Children Act Advisory Committee Annual Report 1992/93 LCD p 46.

FIGURE TWO: TRANSFER STRUCTURE UNDER
THE CHILDREN ACT 1989[7]

HIGH COURT

- exceptional
  cases e.g. where
  a precedent
  could be set

- consolidation
- appropriate to
  hear proceedings
  in the lower court

COUNTY COURT ◄ ◄ ◄ ◄ ◄ ◄ ◄ ◄ COUNTY COURT

- if in the best
  interests of the
  child e.g.
  minimising delay

- consolidation
- appropriate to
  hear proceedings
  in the lower court
  where criterion
  for transfer up no
  longer applies

General
- in the best
  interests of the
  child

Public Law only
- consolidation
- urgency
- exceptional
  complexity,
  gravity or
  importance

MAGISTRATES ◄ ◄ ◄ ◄ ◄ ◄ ◄ ◄ MAGISTRATES
COURT   COURT

- if in the best
  interests of the
  child e.g.
  minimising delay

---

7   Adapted from The Children Act Advisory Committee Annual Report 1991/92 LCD p 23.

Proceedings can be transferred back from a county court level to a family proceedings court if the criteria for transfer upwards no longer apply. Cases can be transferred between the county court level and the High Court on the basis that they are exceptional cases where precedents could be set. The transfer of cases both to the county court and from the county court to the High Court have been affected by practice directions that have been issued indicating that certain categories of cases should be heard at a particular level of court, e.g. child-initiated proceedings should be heard initially in the High Court. Guardians ad litem may need to seek advice from solicitors regarding further practice directions that may be made in this respect. Conversely, cases can transfer back from the High Court to the county court in order to consolidate matters, or where the case would be more appropriately dealt with at the county court level.

The complexity of a particular case may be judged by:

- the issues to be resolved regarding the likelihood of significant harm;
- differing interpretations of an explanation for serious injuries or medical problems;
- the level of risk to the child;
- the anticipated length of hearing;
- areas of disagreement between expert witnesses.

The guardian ad litem needs to make a judgment about the complexity of the case and then make appropriate representations to the court concerning the need for transfer. New events may require this issue to be reconsidered during the currency of proceedings. This matter should be reviewed with the solicitor for the child. It should be noted that cases are allocated new court numbers when transfer between court is effected.

The question of length of hearing arises because it may be difficult for magistrates' courts to make the necessary arrangements for magistrates to sit for more than three days consecutively[8] to hear a case, as well as provide reasons after having heard a large amount of evidence. If the guardian ad litem believes that the case is, by the above standards, uncomplicated but that the hearing might take more than three days, then judgment has to be exercised in considering the representations to be made regarding transfer.

Bearing in mind the delay principle and the need for the case to be heard as quickly as possible once it is prepared for final hearing, the guardian ad litem may wish to check whether the case would be heard any earlier in a county court. If the case were to be heard much later, this may provide a reason for recommending that the case be heard in the magistrates' court, even though it may take four or five days providing the magistrates were able to sit on consecutive days.[9].

---

8   Re H [1992] 2 FLR 330.
9   The Children Act Advisory Committee Annual Report 1993/4 LCD p 50.

Attendance of the child

The guardian ad litem may need to advise the court at an earlier directions appointment about the implications for the final hearing if it is decided that the child should attend. The implications for the court hearing of having a child present can be significant not only for the child, but also for the manner in which other parties and the court conduct themselves. Judges are instinctively opposed to this and will require carefully reasoned advice from the guardian ad litem or the solicitor for the child, if the child is giving instruction directly before allowing it.

The guardian ad litem may feel it appropriate for a child to attend part of the hearing or therapeutically advantageous for the child to meet the judge or magistrates making the decision either before or after they have taken the decision or both.

A child, particularly a teenager, may be judged sufficiently competent to give instruction to a solicitor, and he may wish to be present at the hearing. The guardian ad litem has a duty to advise whether it is in his best interests, regardless of what the child has to say.

Courts may well take the view that it is not particularly helpful for a child to hear unpleasant things about himself or his family and therefore the guardian ad litem should state clearly the reasons why attending court might be in the child's interests in a particular case.

The guardian ad litem should bear in mind the potential ordeal which the child may suffer by sitting in court and listening to criticism of their parents and intimate details about themselves.

Avoiding delay

The guardian ad litem's role in ensuring that a case is prepared fully for a final hearing, and thereby helping avoid delay, may extend beyond the specific areas covered by directions hearings.

In situations where there are parallel civil and criminal proceedings, the guardian ad litem will need to be proactive with members of the wider multi-disciplinary and multi-agency team working with the case. This is to ensure there is no impediment to the progress of the child's case, between the civil proceedings and any criminal matters that are linked with those civil proceedings. This may arise where there are allegations of sexual abuse and the alleged perpetrator is awaiting a criminal trial. Inevitably there will be tensions surrounding what therapeutic help can or cannot be provided to the child whilst awaiting the criminal hearing. The guardian ad litem may need to suggest that the local authority convenes a multi-agency, multidisciplinary meeting to bring together the various professionals involved, and establish whether some agreement can be reached that enables the child's case to be dealt with appropriately.

The guardian ad litem may be aware that there are relatively few issues separating the parties in the matter and that if they were resolved the case might not need a lengthy hearing at court. This could avoid the inevitable conflicts that arise through a contested hearing. The guardian ad litem should be prepared to take the initiative and suggest a meeting between advocates for the various parties, to examine the scope for resolving differences. The guardian ad litem must ensure that any resolution of difference is not at the expense of the child's interests. The guardian ad litem's role is not that of a mediator because, throughout, her prime concern remains the welfare of the child. However where it is judged by the guardian ad litem that any agreements might be in the child's interests, it is right to pursue them.

CHAPTER 10
INTERIM HEARINGS

Introduction

At interim hearings the court may make an interim order: an interim care order, interim supervision order[1] or a section 8 order. An interim care or supervision order can be granted in the first instance for a maximum of eight weeks and thereafter for a maximum of four weeks at a time.

The guardian ad litem should attend all interim hearings unless otherwise excused by the court. The court will look to the guardian ad litem for advice about a range of matters especially the evidence it has heard and any reports that it has received.

The interim hearing

Court rules permit an application to be made for an interim order. At an interim hearing this application may be contested. The court may make an interim order with the consent of the parties. In public law proceedings the court must hear evidence to establish that the threshold criteria are likely to be satisfied[2].

The court has the power to make an interim order before the final hearing of the application of a care order or a supervision order is heard, where the proceedings have been adjourned or where a direction has been made to the local authority to carry out an investigation under section 37(1).

If leave is given by the court, a party may apply for an interim order at a directions appointment. If leave has not been given the application must be made on notice. The application may be made with the consent of all the parties[3]. If it is not agreed the court must fix a hearing, giving at least two days notice to the parties[4], unless the court abridges the notice period[5].

Interim orders may be made on a second or subsequent interim order application in the absence of the parties where a direction has been

---

1   See chapter 18 – Interim care and supervision orders.
2   Newham London Borough Council v AG [1993] 1 FLR 281.
3   FPC (CA 1989) R 1991, r 14(5)(c) and FPR 1991 r 4.14(3)(c).
4   FPC (CA 1989) R 1991, r 14(7) and FPR 1991 r 4.14(5).
5   FPC (CA 1989) R 1991, r 8(8) and FPR 1991 r 4.8(8).

given that the parties should file a written consent prior to the application, provided[6]:

- a written application has been made, to which other parties and the guardian ad litem have consented in writing, and
- the order is the same as the previous order made in the same proceedings.

Order of proceedings

The order in which parties give evidence at interim hearings is the same as at a full hearing[7].

Interim reports

An interim report should, where possible, be prepared by the guardian ad litem for interim hearings where the matters are contested[8]. Contested interim hearings often take place soon after the guardian ad litem has been appointed and, therefore, the guardian ad litem may be in a position to advise the court only to a limited extent. The guardian ad litem may have had the benefit of reading assessments or reports prepared on behalf of the parties.

Interim reports should address only the issues to be decided at the interim hearing and not issues which are only to be decided at the final hearing[9]. The guardian ad litem, in her interim report, should discuss the issue of timing and when the case is likely to be ready for final hearing. If she is not able to say when it is to be ready, then she should give reasons for this. She should consider whether or not any additional experts' reports are necessary. The guardian ad litem should be cautious about making any definitive recommendation, taking into consideration that factors in the case can change by the time the case is ready for final hearing. The initial care plan that will have been prepared by the local authority may change by the time the case is ready for final hearing.

---

6   FPC (CA 1989) R 1991, r 28.
7   See chapter 11 – Final hearing.
8   Hampshire County Council v S [1993] 1 FLR 559; see chapter 18 – Interim care and supervision orders.
9   A v M and Walsall Metropolitan Borough Council [1994] 1 FLR 606.

CHAPTER 11
FINAL HEARING

Introduction

A final directions hearing will be used by the court and the parties to finalise their estimate of the amount of time required to hear the case. By the time the last directions are given all reports should be available, statements lodged and all parties ready to proceed.

The guardian ad litem and her solicitor should meet before the final hearing to iron out any last minute problems which could cause them to review their plans.

Preparing for the final hearing

The guardian ad litem and the solicitor for the child should:

- prepare the child for the final hearing, even if he is not to attend;
- advise the child, subject to his age and undertanding, how the court is going to come to its decision;
- consider the child's attendance at court if no decision has been taken thus far;
- explain to the child, if it is decided that he should attend, how the court operates, who speaks at what times and the order in which the parties present their cases;
- consider the possibility of the child visiting the court (where it is appropriate and if time permits) so that he is not intimidated by the surroundings on the day of the hearing. This can also be useful to a child who is not to attend the final hearing, but who may benefit from a fuller understanding of the proceedings and a sense of participation without having to attend the hearing. Such visits can be arranged with the assistance of the court staff to take place after the day's business in court has concluded;
- decide on the witnesses to be called;
- consider whether the child's views have changed;
- determine the appropriateness of the child attending the final hearing and the child's views on the matter;
- check that all reports have been lodged with the court and distributed to the parties;
- consider the possibility of an adjournment if it is felt appropriate;
- ascertain whether a chronology has been prepared and includes the significant dates and events in the child's life. This chronology is usually prepared by the applicants, but it is a matter to be agreed between the parties, or directed by the court;

- find out what evidence is to be called. If the guardian ad litem is aware that relevant evidence is not being called by the parties, she should consider with the child's solicitor whether such evidence should be called on the child's behalf;
- decide whether or not it is necessary to apply for a witness summons with regard to any of the witnesses who may be reluctant to attend court, or who need a summons for professional reasons, e.g. health visitor or police officer. The most appropriate time to ask for a witness summons is at a directions hearing or at an interim hearing;
- review whether there is any conflict between the instructions being given by the guardian ad litem and those of the child, if the child is of an age and is thought by the solicitor to be capable of giving instructions;
- decide whether arrangements need to be made to keep the child separate from any parties at court;
- decide the appropriateness of using counsel.

Seating arrangements for the final hearing

Seating arrangments vary from court to court. Traditionally the solicitor or barrister for the child must sit on the front bench with the other legal representatives whilst the guardian ad litem, the local authority social worker and other parties sit behind their respective legal representatives. Nowadays, however, the guardian ad litem usually sits beside the child's legal representative. Most courts attempt to adopt a format that is as informal as possible in Children Act proceedings, subject to the nature of the case and physical constraints of the court.

In most family proceedings courts all parties remain seated throughout the hearing, including advocates and witnesses. If practice in a particular court is unfamiliar to a guardian ad litem, then she should enquire of the child's solicitor or justice's clerk.

Commencement of the hearing

On arrival at court the guardian ad litem should make her presence known to the court usher or court clerk. The guardian ad litem should be careful not to appear too familiar with either party or to jeopardise the guardian ad litem's independent position. The justices' clerk or the applicant's advocate will introduce the other legal representatives, the parties and the guardian ad litem to the magistrates or judge.

Oral evidence

The guardian ad litem should be present in court for the duration of the proceedings and she should advise the solicitor on any matters raised in the evidence of any witnesses.

The court may give directions as to the order of the evidence and speeches. This will either be given at the final directions hearing or commencement of the final hearing. In general terms the court will be flexible when scheduling the evidence to be given by expert witnesses. The courts will often allow witnesses to give evidence out of sequence to avoid inconvenience. Many judges will, in a longer case, invite experts of the same discipline to give evidence in sequence so that areas of evidence remain fresh in the mind. However, it must be borne in mind that the volume of evidence that the court has to hear is in most contested cases very large. It is not conducive to a proper hearing for witnesses to be interposed, or to give their evidence discontinuously. If a specific direction is not given then the order for giving evidence will be as follows:

- the applicant;
- any party with parental responsibility;
- other respondents;
- the guardian ad litem;
- the child, if there is no guardian ad litem.

If the child is to give evidence, he will normally do so last, although as already stated the court has the power to vary the order as it thinks fit, particularly if a guardian ad litem is separately represented.

Advice about giving evidence in court can be found in chapter eight of this guide[1].

At the end of the hearing

When making its final order, or refusing the application, the court must state any finding of facts and the reasons for its decision. Not all family proceedings courts will give their reasons in writing immediately after delivering their judgment. A judge is not obliged to put a reasoned oral judgment into writing, because the judgment will be recorded in court. It is important that the solicitor takes notes of the judgment, in case it is decided to appeal the decision.

By the end of the final hearing the child should be prepared fully by the guardian ad litem and solicitor about the possible outcomes, to minimise the risk that the child is surprised by the order or observations made by the magistrates or judge.

The end of the case means that unless there are any outstanding applications which are specified proceedings, the guardian ad litem and the solicitor have discharged their duty and their involvement ends. Efforts should be made to ensure that the child is prepared for the departure of the guardian ad litem and solicitor. In long running cases the child will have formed a relationship with the guardian ad litem and the solicitor and the termination of this relationship should be dealt with sensitively.

---

1   See chapter 8 – Evidence.

If the final order is not in accordance with the guardian ad litem's recommendation, she may consider lodging an appeal on behalf of the child after consulting with the child's solicitor[2]. In addition, if the child has been giving direct instructions to his solicitor it will be necessary for the solicitor to discuss with the child the issue of a possible appeal.

If an appeal is lodged by the guardian ad litem, or any party, the guardian ad litem remains appointed until the appeal is heard. If a court goes against the advice of a guardian ad litem then it must always set out, with clarity, its reasons for so doing otherwise there may be grounds for an appeal[3].

Meeting the child after the final hearing

Subject to the child's age and understanding the guardian ad litem and child's solicitor should meet him after the hearing to discuss the court's decision and reasoning.

In the event of a care order being made, the solicitor and the guardian ad litem should also talk to the child about the statutory reviews where the child's case will be reviewed on a six monthly basis. Further, the guardian ad litem and solicitor should inform the child of the complaints procedure for children in care, which local authorities must provide under section 26.

The guardian ad litem and solicitor should explain to the child that he has the right to come back to court to apply for discharge or variation of the order, including contact and of the circumstances in which it might be appropriate to do so.

Finally, the guardian ad litem and the child's solicitor, taking into consideration the age and understanding of the child, should ensure that the child knows how to contact his solicitor should he so wish.

Once the final hearing has been completed and the child has been seen, the guardian ad litem's role ends, unless an interim order for contact has been made or an appeal has been lodged.

---

2   See chapter 12 – Appeals.
3   North Yorkshire County Council v G and others [1994] 1 FLR 737.

CHAPTER 12
APPEALS AND JUDICIAL REVIEW

Introduction

Appeals and judicial reviews are matters upon which the guardian ad litem must be advised by a solicitor. Appeals are likely to relate to the law and its application rather than to matters of evidence.

Any party to proceedings brought under the Children Act 1989 has a right of appeal:

- if the case is in the family proceedings courts, appeal lies, subject to certain limited exceptions, to the High Court Family Division;
- if the case is in the county court or High Court, appeal lies to the Court of Appeal Civil Division.

Appeals

Appeals are of two types:

- against the decision of a court not to make an order;
- against the decision of a court which has made a particular order.

Leave to appeal is not required where the proceedings are concerned with residence, education or welfare of the child, nor where the appellant has been refused all contact with the child.

An appeal is not a re-trial, and almost invariably proceeds to the basis of the evidence before, and the findings of fact of, the court which heard the matter. There are certain exceptions to this rule, about which the guardian ad litem will require legal advice.

Those who can appeal:

- local authority;
- other parties;
- guardian ad litem on behalf of the child;
- the child.

Possible decision of the Appellate Court

The appellate court may:

- allow the appeal and substitute its own (final) order;
- dismiss the appeal;

- allow the appeal but have insufficient information to enable it to decide what order, if any, should replace that made by the court below; it will then remit the case to the original court or the appropriate level of court for further consideration and determination. The court will give such directions or make such interim orders as are required to promote or safeguard the child's welfare in the meantime.

How to appeal

In the case of a decision of the family proceedings court or a decision by a district judge where an appeal lies to the judge of the same court, a notice of appeal must be filed and served within 14 days after the case[1]; unless it is an appeal against an interim care or supervision order, in which case it must be filed within seven days.

It is necessary to file with the court, serve on the parties and any guardian ad litem, a notice of appeal in writing setting out the grounds upon which the appellant is relying[2].

In the case of a decision of the county court or the High Court, notice of appeal must be given within 28 days.

The guardian ad litem's solicitor will advise her on all aspects of the procedure.

Grounds for appeal

The grounds for appeal should be discussed between the solicitor for the child and counsel, if counsel was involved in the original proceedings or is to be instructed for the appeal, in consultation with the guardian ad litem. Counsel may prepare an "opinion" advising on the merits of an appeal, if that is necessary for legal aid purposes. The grounds for appeal will usually be drafted by counsel.

The Court of Appeal will only interfere if:

- there is an error of law; or
- the court has taken some matter into account which it should not have done, or has ignored some matter that it should have considered; or
- the court's decision is "plainly wrong".

The Court of Appeal will not substitute its own view merely because its members may themselves have reached a different conclusion unless one of the above grounds is made out.

---

1   FPR 1991 r 4.22(3)(a).
2   FPR 1991 r 4.22(2)(a).

Judicial review

Judicial review is the procedure which enables the High Court to review and supervise the actions and decisions of bodies carrying out administrative functions, whether of an executive or judicial nature, e.g. the actions of a local authority, lower courts, and tribunals. The decision may be challenged on the grounds that the action is illegal, irrational or the body has acted with procedural impropriety.

The court has the power to quash the decision taken or order that the matter be re-examined.

Judicial review is concerned with examining the decision making process and not the merits of the case. It is not a process of appeal but a supervisory function of the court.

Judicial review is not a common course of action in child care cases, and therefore if it is contemplated it should be fully discussed with the solicitor for the child and counsel.

PART 4

SPECIFIED PROCEEDINGS

CHAPTER 13
GENERAL PRINCIPLES UNDER THE CHILDREN ACT 1989

Introduction

The Children Act 1989 has simplified the law relating to children and provides certain principles which should be applied to the protection, care and upbringing of children. They are that:

- the welfare of the child is paramount;
- delay is prejudicial; and
- no order should be made unless it is better for the child.

The Act introduced the concept of parental responsibility.

The welfare of the child is paramount

The Children Act 1989 is a piece of legislation whose objective is to promote and protect the welfare of children and in determining any question in regard to the child, the child's welfare should be the court's paramount consideration[1]. When determining the most appropriate course of action for the court to follow in any application under Part IV of the Act or any opposed application for a section 8 order[2], due consideration must be given to the welfare check-list[3].

The welfare check-list

- *the ascertainable wishes and feelings of the child concerned (considered in the light of his age and understanding);*
- *his physical, emotional and educational needs;*
- *the likely effect on him of any change in his circumstances;*
- *his age, sex, background and any characteristics of his which the court considers relevant;*
- *any harm which he has suffered or is at risk of suffering;*
- *how capable each of his parents, and any other person in relation towhom the court considers the question to be relevant, is of meeting his needs;*
- *the range of powers available to the court under the Act in the proceedings in question.*

---

1   CA 1989 s 1(1).
2   CA 1989 s 1(4).
3   CA 1989 s 1(3).

Reducing delay

The Children Act[4] states:

> *"in any proceedings in which any question with respect to the upbringing of a child arises, the court must have regard to the general principle that any delay is likely to prejudice the welfare of the child".*

The "no order" principle

The court when dealing with a case involving a child must not make any order unless it considers that doing so would be better for the child than not making any order at all[5]. If the child's welfare is not going to benefit from the making of any order, then no order should be made.

Parental responsibility

The Children Act 1989 promotes the idea that parents are the best people to bring up a child without the involvement of the court. The Children Act introduced the concept of "parental responsiblity". This concept is defined[6] as *"all the rights, duties, powers, responsibilities and authority which by law a parent of a child has in relation to the child and his property"*.

The following may acquire parental responsibility:
- the child's mother[7] always has parental responsibility for her child (except where a freeing for adoption or adoption order has been made);
- the child's father if he was married to the child's mother at the time of the child's birth[8] or where he was deemed to have been married to the child's mother at the time of birth[9];
- the child's unmarried father where he has entered into a formal parental responsibility agreement with the child's mother[10], obtained a court order for parental responsibility[11] or a residence order[12];
- a person who obtains a residence order (this includes step-parents)[13];
- a testamentary guardian[14];
- a local authority that holds a care order or interim care order in respect of the child[15];

4	CA 1989 s 1(2).
5	CA 1989 s 1(3).
6	CA 1989 s 3(1).
7	CA 1989 s 2(1), (2).
8	CA 1989 s 2(1).
9	CA 1989 s 2(3).
10	CA 1989 s 4(1)(b).
11	CA 1989 s 4(1)(a).
12	CA 1989 s 12(1).
13	CA 1989 s 12(2).
14	CA 1989 s 5(1), (7)(a), (7)(b).
15	CA 1989 s 33(3).

- a person who obtains an emergency protection order (only for the duration of the order)[16];
- adopters[17] and adoption agencies[18].

16   CA 1989 s 44(4)(c).
17   Adoption Act 1976 s 12(3), 25(1), 55(1).
18   Adoption Act 1976 s 18(5).

CHAPTER 14
EMERGENCY PROTECTION ORDER (s 44 & s 45)

Introduction

The making of an emergency protection order confers upon the applicant parental responsibility for the duration of the order[1]. The applicant should exercise that parental responsibility only in the following restricted manner: to safeguard and promote the welfare of the child; where necessary to remove the child to accommodation provided; or to prevent the child's removal from his present accommodation.

Effect of an emergency protection order

While an order under this section ("an emergency protection order") is in force it –

    (a) operates as a direction to any person who is in a position to do so to comply with any request to produce the child to the applicant;

    (b) authorises—

        (i) the removal of the child at any time to accommodation provided by or on behalf of the applicant and his being kept there; or

        (ii) the prevention of the child's removal from any hospital, or other place, in which he was being accommodated immediately before the making of the order; and

    (c) gives the applicant parental responsibility for the child.

                      (CA 1989 s 44(4))

The specific duties placed upon the applicant while an emergency protection order is in force are:

- only to remove the child or prevent the child's removal if it is to safeguard or promote his welfare (section 44(5)(a));
- only to take such action as is reasonably required to safeguard or promote the child's welfare (section 44(5)(b));
- to return the child or allow him to be removed during the period of the order if it appears safe to do so (section 44(10)(a)(b));
- to allow reasonable contact with the child's parents, any other person who has parental responsibility or with whom he was living immediately before the order was made or any holder of a contact

---

[1]   CA 1989 s 44(4)(c).

order and any person acting on behalf of any of those persons (section 44(13));

- to comply with any directions contained within the order and comply with any regulations made by the Secretary of State (section 44(5)(c))[2].

Where the applicant discovers during the course of an emergency protection order that either the child is safe or that circumstances have changed, it is possible for the child to be left in or returned to the care of a parent or the person with whom the child living. It is equally possible for the child to be removed again if the circumstances change, within the scope of the original order if still within the period of the order.

Duration of an emergency protection order

The duration of an emergency protection order is limited to eight days. Before the date of expiry of the order the applicant should apply for any other order such as an interim care order or, in certain circumstances, apply for an extension of the emergency protection order. Such an extension can last for a maximum of seven days only. Where the eighth day is a non-business day, i.e. Saturday, Sunday, Christmas Day, Bank Holiday, then the "eighth" day is the following business day. For example, if the eighth day happened to fall on Good Friday, the next business day when the matter should be heard would be the following Tuesday[3]. The court can fix the duration of an emergency protection order for less than eight days if it feels that to be appropriate.

Who may apply for an emergency protection order

The following may apply for an emergency protection order:

- any person[4];
- local authority;
- authorised person (i.e. NSPCC) or any person authorised by the Secretary of State[5];
- a police officer who is a 'designated officer' where a child is in police protection[6].

Where an emergency protection order has been obtained other than by a local authority, or by a local authority which is not the authority in whose area the child ordinarily lives, the local authority for the area where the child ordinarily lives should consider whether it would be in the child's interests to take over the order[7].

---

2   The Emergency Protection Order (Transfer of Responsibilities) Regulations 1991, (SI 1991/1414).
3   FPC (CA 1989) R 1991 r 1(2) and FPR 1991 r 1.5(6).
4   CA 1989 s 44(1).
5   CA 1989 s 31(9).
6   CA 1989 s 46(7).
7   CA 1989 s 52(3); The Emergency Protection Order (Transfer of Responsibilities) Regulations 1991, (SI 1991/1414).

Applications

The Children Act 1989 provides that applications can be made *ex parte*, i.e. without giving notice. In such situations the applicant is required[8] to serve a copy of the application on each respondent within 48 hours of the making of the order. Where an order is made *ex parte*, any respondent may apply to the court for the order to be discharged upon expiry of a period of 72 hours from its commencement.

For the application to be heard *inter partes* (i.e. after notices have been sent to all parties), one day's notice is required for service of the application upon respondents. The court has discretion to shorten the notice periods. Where there has been an *inter partes* hearing for an emergency protection order, no person who was present at that hearing will be allowed to apply to discharge the order. There is no appeal against the making or refusal to make an emergency protection order[9].

The persons who are entitled to be respondents in such are hearing are:

- the child;
- anyone who has parental responsibility or had it immediately prior to the making of a care order.

In addition notice must be given to:

- every person whom the applicant believes to be a parent of the child;
- any local authority providing accommodation for the child;
- any person with whom the child is living at the time the proceedings are commenced;
- if the child is thought to be living in a refuge[10] (for children at risk), the person providing the refuge.

Applications for an emergency protection order are normally made in the family proceedings court but may be made in the county court or High Court if proceedings are pending relating to the child[11]. There is no provision for the transfer of an emergency protection order application.

Upon the making of an emergency protection order, a copy of the order must be served upon the child, subject to any direction of the justices' clerk or the court, by either serving the order upon the child's solicitor or, where there is no solicitor, a guardian ad litem or, and only with leave of the court or clerk, upon the child.

An application to extend an emergency protection order is a separate application and requires the reappointment of the guardian ad litem. In the event that an extension of an emergency protection order is granted for a further seven days, no applications for discharge can be made within the extended period.

---

8   FPC (CA 1989) R 1991, r 4(4) and FPR 1991, r 4.4(4).
9   CA 1989 s 45(10).
10   Refuge certified under CA1989 s 51(1),(2).
11   Children (Allocation of Proceedings) Order 1991 (SI 1991/1677), art 3(1),(2),(3) and (4).

Grounds for the making of an emergency protection order

The grounds for the making of an emergency protection order are found in section 44(1) which states:

> *Where any person ("the applicant") applies to the court for an order to be made under this section with respect to a child, the court may make the order if, but only if, it is satisfied that –*
>
> > *(a) there is reasonable cause to believe the child is likely to suffer significant harm if –*
> >
> > > *(i) he is not removed to accommodation provided by or on behalf of the applicant; or*
> > >
> > > *(ii) he does not remain in the place in which he is then being accommodated;*
> >
> > *(b) in the case of an application made by a local authority –*
> >
> > > *(i) enquiries are being made with respect to the child under section 47(1)(b); and*
> > >
> > > *(ii) those enquiries are being frustrated by access to the child being unreasonably refused to a person authorised to seek access and that the applicant has reasonable cause to believe that access to the child is required as a matter of urgency; or*
> >
> > *(c) in the case of an application made by an authorised person –*
> >
> > > *(i) the applicant has reasonable cause to suspect that a child is suffering, or is likely to suffer, significant harm;*
> > >
> > > *(ii) the applicant is making enquiries with respect to the child's welfare; and*
> > >
> > > *(iii) those enquiries are being frustrated by access to the child being unreasonably refused to a person authorised to seek access and the applicant has reasonable cause to believe that access to the child is required as a matter of urgency.*
> >
> > *(CA 1989 s 44(1))*

In addition to the grounds set out in section 44 the principles outlined in section 1(1) and (5), namely the paramountcy of the child's welfare and the no order principle, apply. The welfare check-list does not apply.

Section 44(1)(a) embraces all applications and it requires the court to have reasonable cause to believe the child is likely to suffer significant harm. In circumstances where the local authority or authorised person (i.e. NSPCC) applies, as outlined in section 44(1)(b) and (c), it is for the applicant to demonstrate it has reasonable cause to suspect a child is suffering or is likely to suffer significant harm.

The main features of emergency protection orders are summarised in Department of Health Guidance as follows[12]:

---

12   CA 1989 Guidance and Regulations, vol 1: Court Orders, para 4.29 p 51.

- the court has to be satisfied the child is likely to suffer significant harm or cannot be seen in circumstances where the child might be suffering or be likely to be suffering significant harm;
- duration is limited to eight days with a possible extension of seven days;
- certain persons may apply to discharge the order (to be heard after 72 hours);
- the person obtaining the order has limited parental responsibility;
- the court may make directions as to contact with the child and/or medical or psychiatric examination or assessment;
- there is provision for a single justice to make an emergency protection order;
- applications may be made in the absence of any other interested parties (i.e. *ex-parte*), and may, with the leave of the clerk of the court, be made orally;
- the application must name the child, and where it does not, describe the child as clearly as possible.

Guardian ad litem's investigation and report

It is important that the court appoints a guardian ad litem at the earliest possible stage so that the guardian ad litem can both instruct a solicitor and accept service of any application and notices. The guardian ad litem and the child's solicitor will have to consider whether the child is able to instruct the solicitor and consider whether the child would wish to make an application to discharge the emergency protection order.

The short notice of the application will necessarily constrain the investigations of the guardian ad litem and any report she makes to the court. The report is likely to be given orally rather than in writing because of the shortage of time.

The guardian ad litem has to focus on the grounds laid out in section 44(1) (see above), which initially necessitates interviewing the applicant and reading any case files regarding the child. The guardian ad litem could request the applicant to bring the file to court so that they can be read before the hearing.

Depending on the amount of notice given of the hearing and the guardian ad litem's availability, interviews should be conducted with the child who is the subject of the application, his parents and anyone who has care of him. Such interviews may have to be carried out at court prior to the hearing of the matter and the guardian ad litem may have to request a brief adjournment for this purpose.

The guardian ad litem will need to advise the court where ever possible about contact any parties should have with the child and about medical or psychiatric examination or assessment and whether or not the child agrees to such examination or assessment. When the child is capable of instructing the solicitor, the guardian ad litem will need to offer opinion as to whether such examination or assessment could be in the child's interests. Department of Health guidance[13] states:

> "In promoting the welfare of the child, the court can therefore ensure that he is not subjected to unnecessary assessment. As a matter of good practice the local authority should always seek directions on assessment or examination of the child where this is likely to be an issue. Where possible it is anticipated that assessments will be undertaken by professionals agreed between the parties or arranged by the guardian ad litem."

Department of Health guidance indicates that it is not anticipated that the local authority would have carried out all the necessary investigations and its assessment within the 72 hour period. The purpose of the 72 hour period is to give all parties the opportunity to clarify matters, prepare their case and make appropriate representations. The Department of Health guidance[14] states:

> "If an application comes to court for the discharge of an order (emergency protection order) after 72 hours and the assessment has not been completed, the authority will advise the court accordingly. Unless circumstances have so changed as to allay any concerns the authority may have had for the safety of the child, it is unlikely that the court would agree to discharge the emergency protection order."

While an emergency protection order is in force, the child may apply to the court for a direction regarding contact with his parents or any named person. The child can also apply for a variation of a direction as to contact[15]. Similarly the child may apply for a direction as to medical or psychiatric examination or other assessment and for a variation of any such directions given.

The guardian ad litem's involvement terminates upon the making of an order. The guardian ad litem, particularly in circumstances where the child is unable to instruct a solicitor, will need to consider prior to the making of any emergency protection order, whether any applications should be made on behalf of the child before the expiry of any such order the court might make.

---

13   CA 1989 Guidance and Regulations vol 1: Court Orders, para 4.63 p 59.
14   CA 1989 Guidance and Regulations vol 1: Court Orders, para 4.69 p 60.
15   FPC (CA 1989) R 1991, r 2(4)(a) and FPR 1991, r 4.2(4)(a).

CHAPTER 15
CHILD ASSESSMENT ORDER (s 43)

Introduction

Department of Health guidance[1] states that a child assessment order is an order that:

> "deals with the single issue of enabling an assessment of the child to be made where significant harm is suspected but the child is not thought to be at immediate risk (requiring his removal or keeping him in hospital), the local authority or authorised person considers that an assessment is required, and the parents or other persons responsible for him have refused to co-operate. Its purpose is to allow the local authority or authorised person to ascertain enough about the state of the child's health or development or the way in which he has been treated to decide what further action, if any, is required. It is less interventionist than the emergency protection order, interim care order and interim supervision order and should not be used where the circumstances of the case suggest that one of these orders would be more appropriate."

Effect of a child assessment order

A child assessment order can last for up to seven days from the date specified in the order[2]. The order requires any person who is able to produce the child to do so, to enable the assessment (whether medical, psychiatric or social work) in the order to take place. The order will state the nature of the assessment required and the manner in which it is to be undertaken.

In certain circumstances it may be possible for the child to be kept away from home during the course of the assessment[3]. The court must be satisfied that it is necessary for the child to be away from home and therefore specify the length of time. In such circumstances the court will need to make directions regarding the contact the child should have with any other persons during the period.

---

1   CA 1989 Guidance and Regulations vol 1: Court Orders, para 4.6 p 45.
2   CA 1989 s 43(5).
3   CA 1989 s 43(9).

Who may apply for a child assessment order

A local authority or an authorised person may apply for a child assessment order. The guardian ad litem may be appointed upon notice being given to the court of the application by the applicant. Applications must to be made on notice and are therefore *inter partes* applications.

The respondents to an applicant for a child assessment order[4] are:

- every person with parental responsibility;
- the child;
- where the child is subject to a care order, every person who had parental responsibility prior to the making of the care order.

Notice of the application[5] must be sent to:

- the parents;
- every person caring for the child;
- every person who has a contact order in force with respect to the child;
- every person allowed to have contact with the child under section 34;
- any local authority providing accommodation for the child;
- any person with whom the child is living at the time the proceedings are commenced;
- if the child is thought to be living in a refuge[6] (for children at risk) the person providing the refuge.

The application must be made in the family proceedings court[7] unless:

- the application arises out of an investigation of the child's circumstances under section 37(1) in which case it should be made to the court that directed the investigation[8];
- there are other proceedings pending in which case it should be made to the court where the proceedings are pending[9].

Applications may be transferred to the county court and to the High Court.

An application can be made for the child assessment order to be varied by not only the applicants but any of the persons upon whom notice of the proceedings is required to be served[10]. These applications must be made in the court which made the original order[11].

---

4   FPC (CA 1989) R 1991, r 7(1) and FPR 1991, r 4.7(1); FPC (CA 1989) R 1991, Sch 2, column (iii) and FPR 1991 Appendix 3, column (iii).
5   FPC (CA 1989) R 1991, r 4(3) and FPR 1991 r 4.4(3); FPC (CA 1989) R 1991, Sch 2, column (iv) and FPR 1991 Appendix 3, column (iv).
6   Refuge certified under CA 1989 s 51(1),(2).
7   Children (Allocation of Proceedings Order) 1991, (SI 1991/1677), art 3(1).
8   Ibid, art 3(2).
9   Ibid, art 3(3).
10   CA 1989 s 43(11); FPC (CA 1989) R 1991, r 2(3) and FPR 1991, r 4.2(3).
11   Children (Allocation of Proceedings) Order 1991, (SI 1991/1677), art 4(1).

There is a right of appeal against the making of, or the court's refusal to make, a child assessment order. The appointment of the guardian ad litem ends once the court has heard the matter and decided whether to make an order, unless an application is made to vary or discharge any order made[12], in which case a further appointment will be necessary.

No party may make a further application without the leave of the court unless six months has elapsed since the last application[13]. In dealing with any application for a child assessment order, the court may order that no further application may be made by any named person in the order without leave of the court[14].

Grounds for the making of a child assessment order

The child assessment order is primarily for use in situations of non co-operation by parents or carers, and where there is no evidence to indicate the need for any other application. The child assessment order deals primarily with the clearly delineated issue of examination or assessment of a child[15]. The grounds for the making of a child assessment order are to be found in section 43(1), which states:

On the application of a local authority or authorised person for an order to be made under this section with respect to a child, the court may make the order if, but only if, it is satisfied that –

> (a) *the applicant has reasonable cause to suspect that the child is suffering, or is likely to suffer, significant harm;*
> (b) *an assessment of the state of the child's health or development, or of the way in which he has been treated, is required to enable the applicant to determine whether or not the child is suffering, or is likely to suffer, significant harm; and*
> (c) *it is unlikely that such an assessment will be made, or be satisfactory, in the absence of an order under this section.*

(CA 1989 s 43(1))

It is assumed that any application for a child assessment order will have been preceded by an investigation under section 47, where the local authority or authorised person has reasonable cause to believe a child living in their area is suffering or is likely to suffer significant harm. Any court considering an application for a child assessment order, and by implication any guardian ad litem investigating the matter, will wish to be satisfied about the detail of the applicant's investigations concerning the welfare of the child, and that the local authority has taken reasonable steps to persuade the parents or carers to co-operate with any investigation.

---

12   CA 1989 s 43(11),(12).
13   CA 1989 s 91(15).
14   CA 1989 s 91(14).
15   CA 1989 Guidance and Regulations vol 1: Court Orders, para 4.4 p 44.

In addition to the specific criteria laid down for the making of a child assessment order, the court has regard to:

- the paramountcy of the child's welfare (section 1(1));
- the no order principle (section 1(5)).

The court is not required to consider the welfare check-list (section 1(3)), although it is expected to consider factors from the check-list where appropriate.

It is presumed that a child assessment order is to be used to assist in providing basic information about the child's condition precisely because that information is missing, and because efforts to work with parents or carers have failed to produce such information. Where there is sufficient evidence to support an application for either an interim care order, interim supervision order or emergency protection order, then it is these orders which should be sought rather than a child assessment order.

If upon hearing an application for a child assessment order the court believes there are grounds for the making of an emergency protection order, then the court must make that order rather than a child assessment order[16]. Accordingly a child assessment order will be used in situations where the harm that is being considered to the child is generally long term and incremental rather than immediate and severe.

At the conclusion of the assessment, the local authority or authorised person will decide, upon receiving the results, whether further applications need to be made before a court, whether further services and assistance should be offered to the family and child[17], or whether no further action is required.

Guardian ad litem's investigation and report

In situations where not enough is known about a child's circumstances to justify other applications, it is possible that any assessment under a child assessment order will need to be multidisciplinary in nature and will require clear planning as to its execution prior to any application to the court. The court will wish to be satisfied as to the purpose of the assessments required and whether they can actually be carried out; and will look to the guardian ad litem for advice.

The guardian ad litem should enquire whether the family would co-operate with an assessment if it were conducted by a professional of their choice who was also acceptable to the local authority, so as to avoid the need for any order. The guardian ad litem should take account of the child's race, religion, language, gender and any special needs when considering both the application and the choice of examiner, and may advise on whether a named person (e.g. a parent) should be present at any assessment or examination.

---

16   CA 1989 s 43(4).
17   CA 1989 s 17.

The court will look to the guardian ad litem for advice about whether the child is of sufficient understanding to take an informed decision as to whether to consent to the assessment or examination being suggested. A child of sufficient understanding may refuse to consent to any examination or assessment ordered by the court[18]. The guardian ad litem will be expected to make a recommendation as to whether:

■   the application should be granted;
■   the child should attend the court hearing;
■   other directions should be made.

In the event of the child being required to be away from home for the period or part-period of any assessment, then the court will look to the guardian ad litem for views relating to contact the child might have with any adult or siblings.

The guardian ad litem's appointment lasts until the court has decided whether to make an order or not and does not extend for the duration of any child assessment order that the court might make.

---

18   CA 1989 s 43(8).

CHAPTER 16
RECOVERY ORDER (s 50)

Introduction

Recovery orders relate to children who are in the care of the local authority, or subject to an emergency protection order, or in police protection, where there is reason to believe that the child has been unlawfully taken from the care of the responsible person, has run away or is staying away or is missing.

Recovery orders can be made *ex parte* or *inter partes*, usually upon short notice. The guardian ad litem may find that she has very little time between her appointment in a recovery order application and the hearing of the application in which to conduct any enquiries.

Children who may be the subject of a recovery order

Where it appears to the court that there is reason to believe that a child to whom this section applies –

> *(a) has been unlawfully kept away or is being unlawfully kept away from the responsible person;*
> *(b) has run away or is staying away from the responsible person; or*
> *(c) is missing.*

the court may make an order under this section ("a recovery order").

(CA 1989 s 50(1))

The children to whom recovery orders may apply[1] are described in section 49(2) below:

This section applies in relation to a child who is –

> *(a) in care;*
> *(b) the subject of an emergency protection order; or*
> *(c) in police protection*

and in this section "the responsible person" means any person who for the time being has care of him by virtue of the care order, the emergency protection order, or section 46, as the case may be.

(CA 1989 s 49(2))

---

1   CA 1989 s 50(2).

Section 46 refers to circumstances where a child is removed and accommodated by the police in case of emergency (a "police protection order").

Usually a guardian ad litem will have previously been appointed if the child is the subject of an emergency protection order. A guardian ad litem would not necessarily be involved in circumstances where the child is in police protection.

Where the child is subject to a care order the rules indicate, in an *inter partes* application, that the child should receive at least one day's notice before the hearing of the application. If the application cannot be served on the child as is likely, a direction should be sought from the court.

Effect of a recovery order

A recovery order –

(a) *operates as a direction to any person who is in a position to do so to produce the child on request to any authorised person;*

(b) *authorises the removal of the child by any authorised person;*

(c) *requires any person who has information as to the child's whereabouts to disclose that information, if asked to do so, to a constable or an officer of the court;*

(d) *authorises a constable to enter any premises specified in the order and search for the child, using reasonable force if necessary.*

(CA 1989 s 50(3))

A recovery order lasts until the child in question has been recovered. A recovery order has effect throughout the United Kingdom[2].

The *authorised person* referred to in section 50(3) means –

(a) *any person specified by the court;*

(b) *any constable;*

(c) *any person who is authorised –*

(i) *after the recovery order is made; and*

(ii) *by a person who has parental responsibility for the child by virtue of a care order or an emergency protection order,*

to exercise any power under a recovery order . . .

(CA 1989 s 50(7))

---

2   CA 1989 s 50 (13),(14); CA 1989 Guidance and Regulations vol 7: Guardians Ad Litem and other Court Related Issues, paras 4.13 – 4.21 p 31.

Who may apply for a recovery order

Applications for a recovery order may only be made by a person who has parental responsibility for the child by virtue of a care order or emergency protection order, usually the local authority, or where the child is in police protection, the designated officer[3].

Applications

Applications must be made in the family proceedings court[4], unless there are other proceedings pending in which case they are made to the court where the proceedings are pending[5].

Applications may be transferred to another court, both vertically and laterally in accordance with the Children (Allocation of Proceedings) Order 1991. Applications to discharge a recovery order must be commenced in the same court which made the original order[6].

Applications may be made *ex parte*[7] or *inter partes*. It is difficult to see how the guardian ad litem could become involved if an application for a recovery order was made *ex parte*, even though the child is an automatic respondent.

Should a child wish to apply for the discharge of a recovery order, a guardian ad litem would be appointed.

Respondents are[8]:

■   all persons who have parental responsibility;
■   where a child is in care, all persons who held parental responsibility prior to the making of the care order;
■   the child;
■   the person who it is believed may have been responsible for the taking or keeping of the child.

Notice of any recovery order application should be served on the following[9]:

■   any local authority providing accommodation for the child;
■   any person caring for the child at the time of the proceedings;
■   if the child is thought to be living in a refuge[10] (for children at risk) the person providing the refuge.

---

3   CA 1989 s 50(4).
4   Children (Allocation of Proceedings) Order 1991 (SI 1991/1677), art 3(1).
5   Ibid, art 3(3).
6   Ibid, art 4(1) as amended by SI 1993/624.
7   FPC (CA 1989) R 1991, r 4(4) and FPR 1991, r 4.4(4).
8   FPC (CA 1989) R 1991, Sch 2, column (iii) and FPR 1991, Appendix 3, column (iii).
9   FPC (CA 1989) R 1991, Sch 2, column (iv) and FPR 1991, Appendix 3, column (iv).
10   Refuge certified under CA 1989 s 51(1),(2).

Refuges for children at risk

Provision is made under section 51 for certain voluntary homes or registered children's homes, local authority or voluntary organisation foster parents to be registered as providing a refuge for children who appear to be at "risk of harm", (i.e. a "safe house" for children on the run). The homes or foster parents should be issued with a certificate by the Secretary of State under this section thus exempting them from the offence provisions of section 49.

A child who is the subject of a recovery order application may allege that he is at risk of harm whilst in the care of the local authority, and feel more secure placed in a refuge[11]. The maximum time a child may remain continuously in a refuge is 14 days[12].

The person providing the refuge is under an obligation to inform the designated police officer[13] as soon as possible and within 24 hours of arrival, of the child's name[14] and his last permanent address[15] and provide a telephone number by which the person providing the refuge can be contacted[16].

The designated officer must inform the "responsible person" that the child is being provided with a refuge, the name of the person providing the refuge and their telephone number[17]. The designated officer may not disclose to any person the address of the place where the refuge is provided[18]. Consequently, the guardian ad litem and solicitor appointed for the child may only be able to establish telephone contact with the person providing the refuge and not even the child unless he consents to speaking with them.

Grounds for the making of a recovery order

Where it appears to the court that there is reason to believe that a child to whom this section applies –

> *(a) has been unlawfully taken away or is being unlawfully kept away from the responsible person;*
> *(b) has run away or is staying away from the responsible person; or*

---

11   Refuges (Children's Homes and Foster Placements) Regulations 1991, (SI 1991/1507).
12   Ibid, art, 3(9).
13   CA 1989 s 46.
14   The Refuges (Childrens Home and Foster Placement) Regulations 1991, (SI 1991/1507), art 3(3)(b).
15   Ibid, art 3(3)(c).
16   Ibid, art 3(3)(a).
17   Ibid, art 3(7)(a)(b).
18   Ibid, art 3(7)(c).

(c) is missing,

the court may make an order under this section ("a recovery order").

(CA 1989 s 50(1))

The court would have to refer to:

- parmountcy of the child's welfare (section 1(1));
- the no order principle (section 1(5)).

Guardian ad litem's investigation and report

As with all specified proceedings, the court should appoint a guardian ad litem unless it is satisfied that it is not necessary to do so in order to safeguard the child's interest[19].

If the application is heard *ex parte*, then the justice's clerk or court will have to consider whether to appoint a guardian ad litem for the purposes of receiving a copy of the application. If the application is to be made *inter partes* it must be anticipated that the guardian ad litem is more likely to be appointed and to make a report to the court. Given the short notice of the application that will be received, it is likely that such a report would have to be made orally.

The guardian ad litem's knowledge of the case may well vary according to whether the guardian ad litem :

- had been appointed in previous proceedings;
- is currently involved in pending proceedings;
- has no knowledge of the case prior to the appointment.

The guardian ad litem should consider the following matters:

- the local authority's understanding of why the child is missing, has run away or has been taken away;
- any danger that the child might be in;
- the attitude of the child's family;
- in circumstances where the child has run away, whether anything might have occurred where he was being cared for that would have caused him to run away;
- concerns about any significant harm the child might come to whilst absent;
- the local authority's care plan;
- the local authority's placement plans upon the child's return.

Where the child has been the subject of an emergency protection order, there may be only limited information available about the child's circumstances.

---

19   CA 1989 s 41(1); FPC (CA 1989) R 1991, r 10(1) and FPR 1991, 4.10(1).

Where the child is the subject of a care order, there may or may not be pending proceedings such as contact or discharge applications. The guardian ad litem should establish whether the child was unhappy in care and whether the child had been expressing a wish to return to a member of the family. There might be concerns that the child might have been involved in an abusive relationship prior to coming into care, and might, because of the nature of that relationship, seek to return to the person who had abused him.

Many children run away from care. The guardian ad litem should fully investigate the reasons for children running away. They may run to family members, friends, to metropolitan centres such as London or to safe houses[20]. The causes of running away could be linked to one of the following:

- dislike of the particular foster home or residential establishment in which they live;
- that they are being abused in a foster home or residential establishment;
- that the child is linked into an abusive network which he wishes to rejoin;
- that the child is in a placement that cannot meet his needs;
- involvement in crime;
- involvement in prostitution;
- a desire to be independent;
- a desire to return to the care of his family or relatives.

In circumstances where the child has run to a refuge, the guardian ad litem should establish the cause of the child running away in order to determine whether there would be any reason for opposing the making of a recovery order.

Recovery order applications are uncommon. They are likely to be made upon short notice affording the guardian ad litem little time to undertake any enquiries. It is likely that the guardian ad litem will not be able to see the child (as he is missing) and that her enquiries will have to focus on the local authority, the child's family and the various professionals involved in the child's care.

---

20   Children in the Public Care, Sir William Utting, Department of Health para 3.56, p 42.

CHAPTER 17
CARE AND SUPERVISION ORDERS (s 31)

Introduction

Applications for care or supervision orders are the most common applications for which a guardian ad litem will be appointed. This chapter describes the law, the legal process and the matters the court is required to consider when deciding whether or not to grant an application for a care or supervision order. Advice about the guardian ad litem's investigation and report in such applications is to be found in chapter four of this guide.

Effect of a care order

Where a care order is made with respect to a child it shall be the duty of the local authority designated by the order to receive the child into their care and to keep him in their care while the order remains in force.

(CA 1989 s 33(1))

While a care order is in force with respect to a child, the local authority designated by the order shall –

(a) have parental responsibility for the child; and

(b) have the power (subject to the following provisions of this section) to determine the extent to which a parent or guardian of the child may meet his parental responsibility for him.

(CA 1989 s 33(3))

Any care order, other than an interim care order, shall continue in force until the child reaches the age of eighteen, unless it is brought to an end earlier.

(CA 1989 s 91(12))

The acquisition of parental responsibility by a local authority under a care order does not displace the parental responsibility of the child's mother, father[1] or testamentary guardian[2]. A care order has the effect of discharging any residence order and therefore anyone who acquired parental responsibility with the residence order[3] will cease to have parental responsibility. A care order gives the local authority the power to determine the extent to which a parent is able to exercise his parental responsibility.

---

1   In the case of the unmarried father, provided he has a parental responsibility order CA 1989 s 4(1)(a) or has entered into a parental responsibility agreement with the child's mother, CA 1989 s 4(1)(b).
2   CA 1989 s 5(6).
3   CA 1989 s 12(2).

A care order does not give the local authority power to:

■   change the religious persuasion of the child[4];

■   consent or refuse to consent to the making of an adoption order[5], or an order freeing the child for adoption[6];

■   appoint a guardian for the child[7];

or, without either written consent of every person who has parental responsibility for the child or leave of the court to:

■   change the child's surname[8];

■   remove the child from the United Kingdom for more than one month[9].

Local authorities' duties to provide accommodation for a child in care

It shall be the duty of any local authority looking after a child –

(a) when he is in their care, to provide accommodation for him; and

(b) to maintain him in other respects apart from providing accommodation for him.

(CA 1989 s 23(1))

The local authorities' duties are subject to section 22(6) which states:

If it appears to a local authority that it is necessary, for the purpose of protecting members of the public from serious injury, to exercise their powers with respect to a child whom they are looking after in a manner which may not be consistent with their duties under this section, they may do so.

(CA 1989 s 22(6))

The local authorities' duties[10] are to:

■   make immediate and long term plans for placement of a child in accordance with the provisions of section 23, which deals with accommodation and maintenance of looked after children;

■   make arrangements for promoting the welfare of the child who is to be placed[11];

■   ascertain the wishes and feelings of the child, his parents and those with parental responsibility[12];

■   give due consideration to those wishes and feelings and the child's religious persuasion, racial origin and cultural and linguistic background[13];

---

4   CA 1989 s 33(6)(a).
5   CA 1989 s 33(6)(b)(ii).
6   CA 1989 s 33(6)(b)(i).
7   CA 1989 s 33(6)(b)(iii).
8   CA 1989 s 33(7)(a).
9   CA 1989 s 33(7)(b),(8)(a).
10   Adapted from Children Law and Practice, Hershman and McFarlane para B221.
11   Arrangements for Placements of Children (General) Regulations 1991, (SI 1991/890), reg 3(1).
12   CA 1989 s 22(4).
13   CA 1989 s 22(5).

- provide accommodation near to his home so far as is reasonably practicable and reasonably consistent with his welfare[14];
- provide accommodation of siblings together so far as is reasonably practicable and reasonably consistent with their welfare[15];
- provide accommodation for a disabled child which is not unsuitable for his particular needs[16];
- make arrangements to enable the child to live with his parents, person with parental responsibility, holder of a residence order or existing order for care and control, or other persons connected with him, unless to do so would be not reasonably practicable or consistent with his welfare (and in accordance with the regulations)[17];
- not place him in accommodation restricting his liberty (secure accommodation) unless the conditions to do so are satisfied[18];
- consult with the local education authority if it is proposed to provide the child with accommodation or to accommodate him where education is to be provided[19];
- keep the required statutory registers and records[20];
- consider any representations (including a complaint) made by any person listed in section 26(3)[21];
- carry out reviews in accordance with the Review of Children's Cases Regulations 1991[22].

Effect of a supervision order

General

While a supervision order is in force it shall be the duty of the supervisior –

(a) to advise, assist and befriend the supervised child;

(b) to take such steps as are reasonably necessary to give effect to the order; and

(c) where –

(i) the order is not wholly complied with; or

(ii) the supervisor considers that the order may no longer be necessary, to consider whether or not to apply to the court for its variation or discharge.

(CA 1989 s 35(1))

---

14 CA 1989 s 23(7)(a).
15 CA 1989 s 23(7)(b).
16 CA 1989 s 23(8).
17 CA 1989 s 23(5); Placement of Children with Parents etc Regulations 1991, (SI 1991/893).
18 CA 1989 s 25(1); see chapter 25 – Secure accommodation.
19 CA 1989 s 28(1),(2).
20 Arrangements for Placement of Children (General) Regulations 1991, (SI 1991/890), reg 8(2).
21 Representations Procedures (Children) Regulations 1991, (SI 1991/894).
22 Review of Children's Case Regulations 1991, (SI 1991/895) reg 2,3.

Parts I and II of Schedule 3 to the Children Act 1989 deal with further matters relating to supervision orders. These are the effects of a supervision order, the powers and duties of the supervisor, and the obligations of the *responsible person* (defined below). The supervisor named in a supervision order will usually be the local authority[23].

Directions to the child

A supervision order may require the supervised child to comply with any directions given from time to time by the supervisor which require him to do all or any of the following things –

    (a) to live at a place or places specified in the directions for a period or periods so specified;

    (b) to present himself to a person or persons specified in the directions at a place or places and on a day or days so specified;

    (c) to participate in activities specified in the directions on a day or days so specified.

                                   (CA 1989 Sch 3, para 2(1))

It shall be for the supervisor to decide whether, and to what extent, he exercises his power to give directions and to decide the form of any directions which he gives.

                                   (CA 1989 Sch 3, para 2(2))

The court has no power to require a supervisor to give directions and no means of enforcing compliance with such directions, save by considering a care order. A supervision order does not bestow upon the supervisor the power to give directions with regard to medical or psychiatric examination or treatment other than in accordance with the order[24].

Conditions attached to the order

The court may attach specific conditions to a supervision order regarding psychiatric and medical examination and treatment[25]. The order may not include a requirement for psychiatric or medical examination unless the court is satisfied that:

- where the child has sufficient understanding to make an informed decision that he consents to its inclusion;
- satisfactory arrangements have been, or can be made, for the examination[26].

Requirements of the responsible person

The *responsible person* is defined in paragraph 1 of Schedule 3 as:

---

23   CA 1989 Sch 3, para 9.
24   CA 1989 Sch 3, para 2(3).
25   CA 1989 Sch 3, paras 4,5.
26   CA 1989 Sch 3, paras 4,5(5).

> (a) any person who has parental responsibility for the child; and
> (b) any other person with whom the child is living
>
> *(CA 1989 Sch 3, para 1)*

The powers of the supervisor to give directions to the responsible person are outlined in paragraph 3 of Schedule 3:

> *With the consent of any responsible person, a supervision order may include a requirement –*
>
> (a) *that he take all reasonable steps to ensure that the supervised child complies with any direction given by the supervisor under paragraph 2;*
> (b) *that he take all reasonable steps to ensure that the supervised child complies with any requirement included in the order under paragraph 4 or 5;*
> (c) *that he comply with any directions given by the supervisor requiring him to attend at a place specified in the directions for the purpose of taking part in activities so specified.*
>
> *(CA 1989 Sch 3, para 3(1))*

> *A direction given under sub-paragraph (1)(c) may specify the time at which the responsible person is to attend and whether or not the supervised child is required to attend with him.*
>
> *(CA 1989 Sch 3, para 3(2))*

A supervision order may, with the consent of the responsible person, impose certain requirements on him or her.

> *A supervision order may require any person who is a responsible person in relation to the supervised child to keep the supervisor informed of his address, if it differs from the child's.*
>
> *(CA 1989 Sch 3, para 3(3))*

Who may apply for a care or supervision order

> *On the application of any local authority or authorised person, the court may make an order –*
>
> (a) *placing the child with respect to whom the application is made in the care of a designated local authority; or*
> (b) *putting him under the supervision of a designated local authority or of a probation officer.*
>
> *(CA 1989 s 31(1))*

A local authority or an authorised person may apply for a care order or supervision order. *Authorised person* means[27]:

■ the National Society for the Prevention of Cruelty to Children and any of its officers;

---

27 CA 1989 s 31(9).

- any persons authorised by the Secretary of State;
- any officer of a body which is authorised by the Secretary of State.

To date no other bodies or persons have been so authorised. Nearly all such applications will be made by a local authority.

Applications

Respondents to any application under section 31 must be served with[28]:

- a copy of the application;
- a notice giving the date, time and place of hearing,

at least three days before the date set for the hearing or directions appointment.

The persons to whom notice should be given must be served with[29]:

- a notice of the proceedings, with the date, time and place of hearing.

Automatic respondents to an application are[30]:

- any person whom the applicant believes to have parental responsibility for the child;
- the child.

The guardian ad litem is required to notify any person whose joinder to the proceedings would be likely to safeguard the interests of the child, of their right to apply to be joined[31]. Such persons might include grandparents, step-parents, siblings or other members of the extended family. It would be unusual for foster parents to be joined as their views would normally be available to the court as witnesses for the local authority or via the guardian ad litem's report[32].

Notices must be serviced upon[33]:

- any local authority providing accommodation for the child;
- any person with whom the child is living at the time the proceedings are commenced;
- where the child is alleged to be staying in a refuge (for children at risk[34]) the person providing the refuge;
- every person whom the applicant believes to be a party to pending relevant proceedings in respect of the same child;
- every person whom the applicant believes to be a parent without parental responsibility for the child.

---

28   FPC (CA 1989) R 1991, r 4(1)(b) and FPR 1991, r 4.4(1)(b).
29   FPC (CA 1989) R 1991, r 4(3) and FPR 1991, r 4.4(3).
30   FPC (CA 1989) r 1991, r 7(1) and FPR 1991, r 4.7(1); and FPR (CA 1989 R 1991, Sch 2 column (iii) and FPR 1991, Appendix 3, column (iii).
31   FPC (CA 1989) R 1991, r 7(2) and FPR 1991, r 4.7(2), see chapter 3 – Powers and duties of the guardian ad litem.
32   Re G (Minors) (Interim Care Order) [1993] 2 FLR 839.
33   FPC (CA 1989) R 1991, r 4(3), Sch 2, column (iv) and FPR 1991, r 4.4(3), Appendix 3, column (iv).
34   Refuge certified under CA 1989 s 51(1),(2).

An application for a care or supervision order may only be withdrawn with the leave of the court[35]. Such an application for withdrawal may be made either:

- orally to the court if the parties and the guardian ad litem are present[36];
- in a written request setting out reasons for the request and filed and served on the parties[37].

The court may grant a written request if the parties consent in writing, the guardian ad litem has had an opportunity to make representations and the court thinks fit[38]. Otherwise the court will fix a date for the hearing of the request giving at least seven days notice to the parties and the guardian ad litem[39].

The requirement that any oral application for the withdrawal of an application for care or supervision orders be made in the presence of the guardian ad litem will not be satisfied if the child's solicitor only is present and/or the guardian ad litem's solicitor (in case of separate representation) and the guardian ad litem is absent[40].

Grounds for the making of a care or supervision order

The conditions for the making of a care or supervision order are known as the threshold criteria and are to be found in section 31(2) and (3) of the Children Act 1989, which state:

A court may only make a care order or supervision order if it is satisfied –

    (a) that the child concerned is suffering, or is likely to suffer, significant harm; and

    (b) that the harm, or likelihood of harm, is attributable to –

        (i) the care given to the child, or likely to be given to him if the order were not made, not being what it would be reasonable to expect a parent to give to him; or

        (ii) the child's being beyond parental control.

(CA 1989 s 31(2))

No care order or supervision order may be made with respect to a child who has reached the age of seventeen (or sixteen, in the case of a child who is married).

(CA 1989 s 31(3))

Definitions of the terms used in the conditions for the making of care or supervision orders are as follows:

---

35   FPC (CA 1989) R 1991, r 5(5) and FPR 1991, r 4.5(1).
36   FPC (CA 1989) R 1991, r 5(3) and FPR 1991, r 4.5(3).
37   FPC (CA 1989) R 1991, r 5(2) and FPR 1991, r 4.5 (2).
38   FPC (CA 1989) R 1991, r 5(4)(a) and FPR 1991, r 4.5(4)(a).
39   FPC (CA 1989) R 1991, r 5(4)(b) and FPR 1991 r 4.5(4)(b).
40   Re F (A Minor) (Care Order: Withdrawal of Application) [1993] 2 FLR 9.

> *"harm" means ill treatment or the impairment of health or development;*
> *"development" means physical, intellectual, emotional, social or behavioural development;*
> *"health" means physical or mental health; and*
> *"ill treatment" includes sexual abuse and forms of ill treatment which are not physical.*
>
> *(CA 1989 s 31(9))*

Both criteria in section 31(2) must be satisfied[41]. The first concerns present or future predicted harm and the second requires the harm, or likelihood of harm, to be attributable to the quality of the parenting of the child or to the child being beyond parental control. Where it has been necessary to take interim measures (for example, an interim care order or series of them) for the protection of the child which have continued until the hearing, the 'present'[42] referred to is the time immediately prior to the first such measures having been taken. Otherwise the 'present' is the date of the hearing. Harm can be ill treatment or the impairment of health or development, and only one of these conditions needs to be satisfied.

The court has to decide that the harm identified is *significant*. It is therefore the task of the guardian ad litem in her report to explain the significance of the harm or likelihood of harm identified and to assess its impact upon the child's wellbeing and overall development.

The significance of any impairment of health or development is to be determined by comparing the child's health or development with that of a similar child. Account needs to be taken of environmental, social and cultural characteristics as well as whether a child has a disability and specific needs and therefore requires special care and attention. The guardian ad litem may need to consider the standard of health and development that it would be reasonable to expect a child with similar attributes to attain and thereby enable a comparison to be made with the child in question[43].

If the harm or likelihood of harm is found to be *significant*, it has to be further demonstrated to the court that harm or the likelihood of that harm to the child is *attributable* either to the care given or likely to be given to the child were an order not made, not being what it would be reasonable to expect a parent to give him, or to the child being beyond parental control[44].

In considering the care that a reasonable parent would give to a child[45], the Department of Health guidance[46] states:

> "The care given to the child has to be compared not with what it would be reasonable to expect *the* parent to give to the child, but

---

41   See Figure III; Grounds for a Care or Supervision Order, at the end of this chapter.
42   Re M (A Minor) (Care Order: Threshold Conditions) [1994] 3 WLR 558.
43   CA 1989 s 31(10).
44   CA 1989 s 31(2)(b).
45   CA 1989 s 31(2)(b)(i).
46   CA 1989 Guidance and Regulations vol 1: Court Orders, para 3.23 p 25.

with what it would be reasonable to expect *a* parent to give him. It follows from 'reasonable' in the text that the hypothetical parent would be a reasonable parent. The actual parents may be doing their best, but are not able to meet the child's particular needs and are unwilling or incapable of making use of appropriate services. The standard of care which it would be reasonable to expect them to give may be very low. The court must compare the care being given to the child in question with what it would be reasonable to expect a reasonable parent to give him, having regard to his needs. If a child has particular difficulties relating to any aspect of his health or development this could require a higher standard of care than for the average child."

The care needed by children with disabilities, or those suffering from chronic illness, who are likely to require a higher standard of care than a healthy child, must be assessed by comparison to the needs of a similar child and not by comparison with the average healthy child. The standard of care expected of the parents in such cases will be higher than normal; consequently great attention must be paid to linking the child's needs with the capacity of his parents to meet those needs. "Care" is not defined in section 31, but is said by the Department of Health[47] to mean:

"providing for the child's health and total development (physical, intellectual, emotional, social and behavioural) and not just having physical charge of the child."

The use of the term *likely* in section 31(2)(b)(i) requires it to be shown that there exists a real, significant risk of significant harm[48], and covers the following situations:

- where a child's standard of care is thought to be deteriorating or persistently too low;
- where the child is not currently being cared for by the parents, but if he were returned to their care, there would be grounds for concern about his welfare.

The term *beyond parental control* in section 31(2)(b)(ii) covers situations where any harm that the child has suffered, or is likely to suffer, can be attributed to a lack of parental control, and not the standard of care being made available to the child. There may be circumstances where it is the very lack of control which prevents the child from benefiting from the standard of care made available.

The grounds for the making of a care or supervision order are summarised in figure three at the end of this chapter.

---

47   CA 1989 Guidance and Regulations vol 1: Court Orders, para 3.23 p 26.
48   Newham London Borough Council v AG [1993] 1 FLR 281.

Decision of the court

If the threshold criteria in section 31(2) are met, the court must have regard to the principles set out in section 1 of the Act, namely that the welfare of the child is the paramount consideration and the presumption that no order should be made unless the court considers that doing so would be better for the child than making no order at all (the "no order" principle)[49].

Welfare check-list

When considering whether to make an order[50], the court must have regard to the welfare check-list outlined in section 1(3). This states:

> *In the circumstances mentioned in subsection (4), a court shall have regard in particular to –*
>
> (a) *the ascertainable wishes and feelings of the child concerned (considered in the light of his age and understanding);*
> (b) *his physical, emotional and educational needs;*
> (c) *the likely effect on him of any change of his circumstances;*
> (d) *his age, sex, background and any characteristics of his which the court considers relevant;*
> (e) *any harm which he has suffered or is at risk of suffering;*
> (f) *how capable each of his parents, and any other person in relation to whom the court considers the question to be relevant, is of meeting his needs;*
> (g) *the range of powers available to the court under this Act in the proceedings in question.*
>
> *(CA 1989 s 1(3))*

Court rules require the guardian ad litem to have regard to (a) – (f) of the welfare check-list, but not to (g). Separately the Rules require the guardian ad litem to advise the court on:

> *the options available to it in respect of the child and the suitability of each such option including what order should be made in determining the application.*
> *(FPC (CA 1989) R 1991, r 11(4)(e))[51]*

Other options available to the court

If the court makes a supervision order or declines to make any care order or supervision order, it can consider making orders as applied for by any of the parties and it also has the option of making various orders (section 8 orders

---

49   CA 1989 s 1(5).
50   CA 1989 s 1(4).
51   FPR 1991 r 4.11(4)(e).

or a family assistance order under section 16) even if formal applications have not been made for them. These are orders "of the court's own motion".

In the event that a court makes a care order the court can, in addition, make a parental responsibility order for an unmarried father who has applied for it, and orders for contact under section 34, whether or not a formal application has been made to the court for such an order.

The only other orders which the court can make of its own motion in conjunction with a care order are orders under section 91(14) and orders under section 6(7)(c) terminating the appointment of a testamentary guardian. Both orders are described below.

The guardian ad litem should always consider whether the child's interest can be served by the making of such orders, and where appropriate, should address them in her report.

The orders which the court can make of its own motion are as follows:

- **Section 8 orders:**

   These are orders specified under section 8 of the Children Act 1989:

   In this Act:

   "a contact order" means an order requiring the person with whom a child lives, or is to live, to allow the child to visit or stay with the person named in the order, or for that person and the child otherwise to have contact with each other;

   "a prohibited steps order" means an order that no step which could be taken by a parent in meeting his parental responsibility for a child, and which is of a kind specified in the order, shall be taken by any person without the consent of the court;

   "a residence order" means an order settling the arrangements to be made as to the person with whom a child is to live; and

   "a specific issue order" means an order giving directions for the purpose of determining a specific question which has arisen, or which may arise, in connection with any aspect of parental responsibility for a child.

   (CA 1989 s 8(1))

   A prohibited steps order can be used, for example, to prohibit someone holding parental responsibility for a child from allowing that child to have contact with a named person (perhaps the alleged perpetrator of abuse).

   A specific issue order can be used to determine matters in dispute between parties who may hold parental responsibility for the child (other than the local authority) such as the education or medical treatment which a child should receive.

■ **Family assistance orders:**

The court can make an order requiring a probation officer or an officer of the local authority to advise, assist and (where appropriate) befriend any parent or guardian of a child who is the subject of the proceedings before the court, and/or any person with whom the child is living or who has a contact order in respect of the child, and/or the child himself.

To make such an order the court must be satisfied that the circumstances of the case are exceptional and that the court has the consent of every person to be named in the order other than the child[52].

A family assistance order can be effective for not more than six months from the date on which it is made[53].

Such orders can be made where, for example, the local authority has been involved with the family up to the date of the final hearing and it is intended that the local authority will take a specified role, by agreement with the family, for a time limited period thereafter; to assist with the negotiation of, or supervision of, contact arrangements with extended family; or where the family have very recently suffered a crisis (such as a family bereavement) with which it is agreed by all parties the local authority can assist by supporting the family in some form.

■ **An order prohibiting further applications without leave of the court:**

The Act provides that the court can order that certain specified applications may not be made with respect to the child concerned by any persons named in the order without the leave of the court[54]. Whilst orders under section 91(14) restricting future applications, should usually only be made in cases with a thread of repeated and near vexatious applications[55], exceptional circumstances might exist in an individual case which justify such an order on a first application.

Such orders are not made lightly but may be considered where, for example, it is thought that a further application by a parent for a contact order or discharge of a care order would be seriously disruptive to the child.

■ **Termination of the appointment of testamentary guardian:**

On the death of a parent with parental responsibility and a formal residence order or on the death of the only surviving parent holding parental responsibility for a child, if that person has appointed by will a

---

52   CA 1989 s 16.
53   CA 1989 s 16(5).
54   CA 1989 s 91(14).
55   Re Y (Child Orders: Restricting Applications) [1994] 2 FLR 699.

person to act as testamentary guardian for the child, the appointment then takes effect. The testamentary guardian then has parental responsibility for the child[56].

The court may however order in family proceedings that the appointment of the testamentary guardian should be brought to an end, thereby ending the parental responsibility given to that person[57].

The order can be used if the testamentary guardian is not though to be an appropriate person to hold parental responsibility for the child. The order can also be used if the effect of other orders to be made by the court on that occasion will be that, in the absence of the termination of the appointment, the testamentary guardian will share parental responsibility with other (including the local authority under a care order) but the sharing of which would not be in the child's best interests.

No order principle

The court, having considered the welfare check-list, will then consider section 1(5) which states:

Where a court is considering whether or not to make one or more orders under this Act with respect to a child, it shall not make the order or any of the orders unless it considers that doing so would be better for the child than making no order at all.

(CA 1989 s 1(5))

Contact

The court must consider proposed contact arrangements before making a care order.

Before making a care order with respect to any child the court shall –

(a) consider the arrangements which the authority have made, or propose to make, for affording any person contact with a child to whom this section applies; and

(b) invite the parties to the proceedings to comment on those arrangements.

(CA 1989 s 34(11))

The court has a duty to consider contact as a specific issue. Whilst the local authority's care plan (if an order is made) commands the greatest respect and contact must not be allowed to destabilise or endanger arrangements for the child, nevertheless the court may require the local authority to justify their long term plans to the extent only that those plans exclude contact between parent and child[58].

---

56 CA 1989 s 5(6).
57 CA 1989 s 6(7)(c).
58 Re B (Minors) (Care: Contact: Local Authority's Plans) [1993] 1 FLR 543.

Guardian ad litem's investigation and report

See chapter four of this guide.

The court will be helped by the guardian ad litem's analysis of all the information she has gathered. In considering the paramountcy of the child's welfare and whether or not to make an order, the guardian ad litem will be expected to assist the court in its duty to scrutinise the local authority's plans[59]. Where the guardian ad litem disagrees with the care plan, she should be ready to advise the court as to what other order (if any) the court might make to secure the result advised by the guardian ad litem. In particular the guardian ad litem should bear in mind that the court has no power to attach conditions to a final care order[60], save by way of contact. Taking into account all the information put before it, the court will consider whether the powers available to it need to be exercised or not.

---

59   Re T (Minor) (Care Order: Conditions) [1994] 2 FLR 423.
60   Ibid; Kent County Council v C [1993] 1 FLR 308; Re B (A Minor)(Care Order: Review) [1993] 1 FLR 421.

FIGURE THREE: GROUNDS FOR A CARE OR SUPERVISION ORDER: CHECK-CHART[61]

---

1. The statutory threshold criteria must first be met, namely, the court must be satisfied:

   (a) that the child concerned is suffering, or is likely to suffer, significant harm; and

   (b) that the harm, or likelihood of harm is attributable to:

      (i) the care given to the child, or likely to be given to him if the order were not made, not being what it would be reasonable to expect a parent to give to him; or

      (ii) the child's being beyond parental control.

---

2. The court will then consider the questions:

   (a) should an order be made?

   (b) if so, what type of order?

   In doing so the court will:

   (a) apply the principle that the child's welfare is the paramount consideration (CA 1989, s 1(1));

   (b) apply the statutory welfare check-list (CA 1989, s 1(3));

   (c) not make an order unless it considers that doing so would be better for the child than making no order at all (CA 1989, s 1(5));

   (d) before making a care order, consider the proposed arrangements for contact with the child and invite comment upon them (CA 1989, s 34(11)).

Care Order	Supervision Order	No Order
■ and/or parental responsibility order (if applied for)	■ and/or parental responsibility order (if applied for)	
■ and/or orders with respect to guardians	■ and/or orders with respect to guardians	
■ contact under s 34	■ and/or a residence order	
	■ and/or any other s 8 order	
	■ and/or financial relief	

---

61   Children Law and Practice, Hershman and McFarlane, Family Law, C 108.

CHAPTER 18
INTERIM CARE AND SUPERVISION ORDERS (s 38)

Introduction

Department of Health guidance[1] states:

> "Interim care and supervision orders are similar in effect to full care and supervision orders[2], except in two particulars; the court determines the duration of the interim order and may give directions to the local authority as to the medical or psychiatric examination of the child or other assessment . . . ".

Who may apply for an interim care or supervision order

Those entitled to apply for care or supervision orders, namely a local authority or an authorised person[3], may apply for an interim care or supervision order when an application for a care or supervision order has been made under section 31.

When the court makes a direction under section 37, an interim care or supervision order may be made by the court of its own motion. The parties in what, at that stage, must be private law proceedings, may suggest such a course of action to the court. No party may apply for an interim care or supervision order under section 37.

In what type of proceedings may an interim care or supervision order be made

Interim care or supervision orders may be made in any proceedings arising from an application for a care or supervision order[4], and in proceedings where the court gives a direction under section 37(1) (as above).

Effect of an interim order

The maximum length of an interim order is initially eight weeks[5] and thereafter four weeks[6]. Where the first interim order is made for less than

---

1   CA 1989 Guidance and Regulations vol 1: Court Orders, para 3.38 p 28.
2   For effect of care order and supervision orders see chapter 17 – Care and supervision orders.
3   CA 1989 s 31(1),(9).
4   CA 1989 s 31.
5   CA 1989 s 38 (4)(a).
6   CA 1989 s 38 (5)(a).

eight weeks the next such order can run for the remainder of the eight week period[7], or four weeks, whichever is longer.

Grounds for the making of an interim care or supervision order

> *A court shall not make an interim care order or interim supervision order under this section unless it is satisfied that there are reasonable grounds for believing that the circumstances with respect to the child are as mentioned in section 31(2).*
>
> *(CA 1989 s 38(2))*

The grounds are therefore:

- reasonable grounds for believing the child is suffering or is likely to suffer significant harm attributable to the quality of parenting, or the child being beyond parental control;

and the court takes into account:

- welfare check-list (section 1(3));
- no order principle (section 1(5)).

The key words in section 38(2) providing the distinction between the grounds for making an interim care or supervision order and the grounds for making a care or supervision order are that the court *is satisfied that there are reasonable grounds for believing*; the court does not have to be satisfied that the grounds for a care or supervision order do in fact exist. Department of Health guidance[8] on this matter states:

> "This test is not the same as for a full order which requires proof that the child is suffering or likely to suffer significant harm. It would not be realistic to require proof of the condition at the interim stage when the guardian ad litem's final report will probably not have been received and all evidence heard".

Bearing in mind its responsibilities under section 1(5) only to make an order if it considers it will be better so to do than making no order at all, the court will have to consider whether any other orders could be made that would ensure the child's protection for the duration of any proceedings. The court might, for example, make an interim residence order[9] in favour of a parent or other person. If the court makes such an order it is also required to make an interim supervision order unless the court is satisfied that the child's welfare will be safeguarded without making such an order[10].

A section 8 order can be made by the court for a specified period at any time during the course of proceedings where it has the power to do so[11].

---

7 CA 1989 s 38 (5)(b).
8 CA 1989 Guidance and Regulations vol 1: Court Orders, para 3.37, p 28.
9 CA 1989 s 11(3).
10 CA 1989 s 38(3).
11 CA 1989 s 11(3),(7).

The court will have to consider:

■ the length of any interim order;
■ contact between the child and members of his family, and any other relevant persons;
■ medical or psychiatric examinations or other assessments.

Where the court has made an interim care or supervision order it may also make an interim contact order[12]. Where the court has made an interim supervision order it may also make a specific issue order, or prohibited steps order[12]. The prohibited steps order might be used as a means of preventing a particular person without parental responsibility having contact with the child when an interim supervision order, has been made instead of an interim care order. A specific issue order cannot be made in order to achieve a result that might otherwise be achieved by the making of a residence or contact order[13].

The court will also need to consider whether any medical or psychiatric examinations or other assessments should be carried out and, if so, when and by whom[14]. Throughout its consideration of all the above matters, the court will be mindful of the child's wishes and feelings and the extent to which the child is capable of making an informed decision about the matters being considered.

The guardian ad litem's investigation and report

The court will expect advice from the guardian ad litem about any alternative orders to an interim care or supervision order that might be made as an interim measure whilst a care application is pending.

The extent to which the guardian ad litem is able to assist the court in any of its considerations regarding the above matters will depend on whether the guardian ad litem was appointed before the hearing and on the amount of time available to the guardian ad litem to begin her investigations prior to the hearing. The guardian ad litem may find herself attending an interim hearing without having been able to interview the child or any of the parties. In these circumstances it may be appropriate for the guardian ad litem to request a brief adjournment so that she might conduct short interviews at the court. The guardian ad litem should bear in mind that the child is unlikely to be at court unless he is old enough to instruct his own solicitor, and therefore unlikely to be available for interview at court.

The guardian ad litem may be asked to give evidence based on her initial investigations to the court about whether an interim care or supervision order should be made. The guardian ad litem may be asked to offer views,

---

12 If the child is the subject of an interim care order, any contact orders made would be under section 34; if the child is the subject of an interim supervision order, any orders regarding contact, a specific issue, or prohibited steps would be under section 8.
13 CA 1989 s 9(5)(a).
14 See chapter 7 – Expert reports.

either orally or in writing or both[15]. The guardian ad litem's prime duty is to safeguard and promote the child's welfare, and this should be her foremost consideration. If the guardian ad litem has not had an opportunity to begin her investigations, any views she might offer at the interim hearing stage would have to be qualified in terms of her knowledge of the case.

The guardian ad litem's advice will be sought about contact whilst the child is subject to an interim care order[16] or interim supervision order[17]. Contact can take the form of face to face contact, but can also include telephone calls and letters. Any decisions taken by the court will necessarily be temporary until either the conclusion of the proceedings or until further order from the court. Judgments will have to be based on the recommendations of the guardian ad litem, and submissions from the local authority and other parties, as to the appropriate level of contact and as to whether any such contact may put the child at risk of harm or might be likely to prejudice any investigations that are currently taking place to ascertain whether the child has suffered significant harm. The court will wish to know of any expressed wishes and feelings of the child. The guardian ad litem may wish to offer advice about whether contact should be supervised and if so, by whom, and about the most appropriate venue for contact.

Contact orders might be sought by the guardian ad litem or the local authority for the purposes of any assessments that will bring the child into contact with any of the parties or someone who it is alleged might have caused the child significant harm. Consideration would have to be given to contact by the child with siblings who may be placed separately or if not the subject of any order, still living at home. Where there are genuine concerns about the child having contact with someone who might have caused him significant harm, it might be possible for the child to have contact with someone else who is familiar to him but who does not pose a risk either directly to the child or to any investigations that are taking place[18].

---

15 FPC (CA 1989) R 1991, r 11(5) and FPR 1991, r 4.11(5); in chapter 8 – Evidence for advice about giving evidence.
16 CA 1989 s 34(11).
17 CA 1989 s 8.
18 See chapter 22 – Contact order.

CHAPTER 19
INVESTIGATION OF THE CHILD'S CIRCUMSTANCES (s 37)

Introduction

Where, in any family proceedings in which a question arises with respect to the welfare of any child, it appears to the court that it may be appropriate for a care or supervision order to be made with respect to him, the court may direct the appropriate authority to undertake an investigation of the child's circumstances.

(CA 1989 s 37(1))

Family proceedings are defined in the Children Act 1989[1] as proceedings under:

- the inherent jurisdiction of the High Court in relation to children;
- Parts I, II and IV of the Children Act 1989;
- the Matrimonial Causes Act 1973;
- the Domestic Violence and Matrimonial Proceedings Act 1976;
- the Adoption Act 1976;
- the Domestic Proceedings and Magistrates Court Act 1978;
- sections 1 and 9 of the Matrimonial Homes Act 1983;
- Part III of the Matrimonial and Family Proceedings Act 1984.
- the Human Fertilisation and Embryology Act 1990, section 30[2].

Who may apply for a section 37 direction

No party may apply for a section 37 direction but parties in any family proceedings may, if they think it appropriate, suggest it to the court as a possible course of action.

When the court gives a direction under this section, the local authority has to consider whether they should:

(a) *apply for a care order or for a supervision order with respect to the child;*

(b) provide services or assistance for the child or his family; or

(c) take any other action with respect to the child.

(CA 1989 s 37(2))

Section 37 further specifies that, where a local authority undertakes such an investigation and decides not to apply for a care order or supervision order, the local authority shall inform the court of:

(a) their reasons for so deciding;

(b) any service or assistance which they have provided, or intend to provide, for the child and his family; and

(c) any other action which they have taken, or propose to take, with respect to the child.

(CA 1989 s 37(3))

The local authority must provide this information to the court, in writing[3], within eight weeks of the date of the direction unless otherwise directed by the court[4]. The court is not empowered to make a care order or supervision order of its own motion, but can make an interim order initially up to a maximum of eight weeks[5]. The local authority have to give reasons for whatever decisions they take as a consequence of their investigations. The child is not able to appeal against the decision of the local authority.

Appointment of guardian ad litem in a section 37 direction

A guardian ad litem can only be appointed under a section 37 direction if an interim care order has been made or if the court is considering making such an order[6]. The proceedings are thus *specified proceedings* by virtue of section 41(6)(b). A guardian ad litem may not be appointed if an interim supervision order has been made unless the court indicates that it is also considering making an interim care order.

The proceedings cease to be *specified proceedings* when the local authority informs the court that it is not going to apply for a care or supervision order[7]. The termination of the appointment of the guardian ad litem should be by judicial rather than administrative act[7]. The question of the guardian ad litem's continuing involvement should be reviewed by the court shortly after the date upon which the section 37 report is due to be received by the court[7].

The guardian ad litem's investigation and report

The guardian ad litem should appoint a solicitor for the child (if he is not already represented). The guardian ad litem should conduct her

---

3   FPC (CA 1989) R 1991, r 27(5) and FPR 1991, r 4.26(5).
4   CA 1989 s 37(4).
5   See chapter 18 – Interim care and supervision orders.
6   CA 1989 s 41(6)(b).
7   Re CE (Section 37 Direction) [1995] 1 FLR 26.

investigations and prepare her report[8] mindful of the threshold criteria in section 31(2) and the welfare check-list in section 1(3).

The guardian ad litem may comment on the other matters set out in section 37(2) and make observations about the services or assistance that the child or his family might require, whether or not the guardian ad litem believes that there are grounds for making an interim care order. The guardian ad litem must also consider whether there are any other actions that the local authority might take with respect to the child (section 37(2)(c)).

These might include whether the local authority, if qualified, should consider applying for leave to apply for a specific issue order or a prohibited steps order[9] under section 8, or whether the child or family should be provided services under section 17[10].

Where the court has made (or is considering making) an interim care order under section 37, the guardian ad litem is unlikely to have been present at court at the making of that order unless she was involved in the family proceedings in which the section 37 direction was made. This situation might arise in proceedings under the Adoption Act 1976. Generally, the court will not have had the benefit of the guardian ad litem's advice regarding matters it is required to consider, eg contact, although it may have received a report from a court welfare officer. The guardian ad litem may need to request a directions appointment to advise the court about such matters[11].

The court has no power to require the local authority to make any application. Where the guardian ad litem feels an application for a care order would be justified but where the local authority does not agree, the guardian ad litem's powers are limited by section 37 of the Children Act 1989[12]. The guardian ad litem, on behalf of the child, has a duty and a professional responsibility to articulate and advocate the child's wishes and feelings, the needs of the child, and identify how best to safeguard and promote the welfare of the child, to the court and also to the local authority.

The guardian ad litem should liaise with the local authority in order to keep the local authority apprised, throughout its investigation, of the matters the guardian ad litem is considering, the wishes and feelings of the child, the needs of the child, and the possible means of best safeguarding and promoting the welfare of the child.

Where the guardian ad litem and the local authority do not agree, the guardian ad litem should, in her report, outline her reasons for disagreeing with the local authority. The parties to the proceedings may wish to

---

8   See chapter 4 – Guardian ad litem's investigations and report, for further advice.
9   Nottinghamshire County Council v P [1993] 2 FLR 134 for restrictions on local authorities applying for a prohibited steps order.
10   CA 1989 s 17, 'Provision for services for children in need, their families and others'.
11   For further advice about the guardian ad litem's duties with respect to an interim care order, see chapter 18 – Interim care and supervision orders.
12   CA 1989 s 37(3).

reconsider what action they might take. The articulation by the guardian ad litem of the child's wishes, feelings and needs might, for example, influence a party to consider whether to apply for a section 8 order in respect of the child.

Where the guardian ad litem is extremely concerned about the local authority not pursuing a particular course of action, she should discuss the matter with her Panel manager before considering whether to make, on the child's behalf, any representations to the local authority under section 26(3)[13].

If the local authority, having undertaken its assessment, decides to apply for a care order or a supervision order, then a guardian ad litem should be appointed[14].

Summary

The guardian ad litem's appointment where a section 37 direction has been made is unusual. The transition from private law proceedings to public law proceedings, with the consequential involvement of the guardian ad litem and the local authority (possibly in addition to the court welfare officer), can easily cause confusion for the child, his family and other professionals.

The guardian ad litem's powers and duties are restricted by the limitations placed upon the court under section 37.

The guardian ad litem must:

■ comment on the local authority's decisions whether to make an application to the court as a result of its enquiries and investigation;
■ consider making representations to the court and to local authority if the local authority makes no application when the guardian ad litem believes that an application is necessary to safeguard and promote the child's welfare.

---

13   CA 1989 s 26(3)(e).
14   See chapters 17 – Care and supervision orders; and, 18 – Interim care and supervision orders.

CHAPTER 20

DISCHARGE OF A CARE OR SUPERVISION ORDER AND VARIATION, SUBSTITUTION OR EXTENSION OF A SUPERVISION ORDER (s 39 & Sch 3 para 6)

Introduction

Upon receiving an application for the discharge of a care or supervision order, or the variation or substitution or extension of a supervision order, the court is required to consider appointing the guardian ad litem who acted in the previous proceedings[1]. Such an appointment will be likely to hasten the progress of the guardian ad litem's enquiries because of her prior knowledge of the case and avoid unnecessary delay in the matter being heard. Applications for a residence order in respect of a child in care also have the effect of discharging a care order and are considered in chapter 21.

Who may apply

The child, the local authority or any person who has parental responsibility for the child may apply for the discharge of a care order[2], or to substitute a supervision order for a care order[3]. Applications for the variation or discharge of a supervision order may be made by the child, the supervisor or any person who has parental responsibility for the child[4].

Circumstances may arise where a child, being the subject of a supervision order, is living with someone who is not entitled to apply for the discharge of the order but who nevertheless is affected by the supervision order and any conditions it implies. In such circumstances the person with whom the child is living is entitled to apply to vary the order in so far as it affects that

---

1   FPC (CA 1989) R 1991, r 10(8) and FPR 1991, r 4.10(8).
2   CA 1989 s 39(1); a residence order in respect of a child in care has the effect of discharging a care order, see chapter 21 – Residence order.
3   CA 1989 s 39(4).
4   CA 1989 s 39(2).

person[5], or seek the court's leave to apply for a residence order, thereby discharging the care order.

Applications may therefore be made by:

- the supervisor, usually the local authority;
- the child;
- anyone with parental responsibility;
- the responsible person with whom the child may be living[6].

Conditions for discharging a care order or substituting a supervision order for a care order

In considering whether to discharge a care order or to substitute a supervision order for a care order, the court does not have to take into account the threshold criteria in section 31(2)[7]. The court considers immediately the welfare of the child as outlined in section 1:

- paramountcy of the child's welfare (section 1(1));
- welfare check-list (section 1(3));
- no order principle (section 1(5)).

The welfare of the child is the *paramount consideration*. A child might not appear to be at risk if he returned to the care of either or both parents or former carers, and yet it would appear to be in the over-riding interests of his welfare for him to remain in care. Those applying for the discharge of the care order or to substitute a supervision order for a care order would need to demonstrate that a change of order or discharge of an order would be more likely to promote his interests and welfare than the status quo. The guardian ad litem will assist the court by considering the welfare check-list in detail and the principle of "no order".

Conditions for the variation or discharge or extension of a supervision order

In considering the discharge or variation or extension of a supervision order the court will focus on whether the child would be better off with the relevant order in place or varied rather than whether the child would be at risk if the order were not to remain in place. The emphasis is therefore on maximising the welfare of the child.

Extension

Supervision orders, initially, can only be made for a period of up to one year[8]. A local authority can apply to extend a supervision order[9]. The

---

5   CA 1989 s 39(3).
6   For definition of 'responsible person' see chapter 17 – Care and supervision orders.
7   CA 1989 s 39(5).
8   CA 1989 Sch 3, para 6(1).
9   CA 1989 Sch 3, para 6(3).

supervision order may not be extended so that it runs for longer than a period of three years beginning with the date on which it was made[10]. During the first year of the order the local authority should always decide whether to apply to extend it. The local authority is not required to prove that threshold criteria still exist.

Variation

Applications to vary a supervision order may relate to:

- the specific obligations upon the responsible person[11];
- specific directions about psychiatric and medical examinations and treatment[12];
- whether the requirements of the supervisor have been met[13].

Regarding medical treatment directed by a supervision order, the Department of Health guidance[14] states:

> "The medical practitioner responsible for the treatment must report in writing to the supervisor if he is unwilling for the treatment to continue for any reason, or if he considers that the treatment should continue beyond the period specified, the child needs different treatment, is not susceptible to treatment or does not require further treatment. The supervisor must refer the report to the court, which may then cancel or vary requirement as to treatment."

It is not possible to vary a supervision order to a care order. To replace the supervision order with a care order the local authority (or other parties to the proceedings) must appeal against the refusal to make a care order, or the local authority can apply for a care order by way of a fresh application.

Discharge

Applications for the discharge of the supervision order may relate to some of the matters outlined above, and/or whether there is a need for the order to remain in being.

In all applications to vary, extend or discharge a supervision order the court will have to consider:

- the paramountcy of the child's welfare (section 1(1));
- the welfare check-list (section 1(3));
- the no order principle (section 1(5)).

Guardian ad litem's investigation and report

On any application to discharge a care order, the guardian ad litem must consider not only whether she agrees or disagrees with the application but

---

10   CA 1989 Sch 3, para 6(4).
11   CA 1989 s 39(3).
12   CA 1989 Sch 3, para 5(7).
13   CA 1989 s 35(1)(c).
14   CA 1989 Guidance and Regulations vol: 1 Court Orders, para 3.94, p 41.

also whether she would wish to recommend the substitution of a supervision order for a care order[15] rather than recommend the discharge of that order. The guardian ad litem should also consider the range of orders available under sections 8 and 16, and whether to recommend that the court makes such an order of its own motion. At the end of her investigations the guardian ad litem will also have to consider whether she believes it would be in the child's interests for the court to exercise its powers to restrict further applications with respect to the child by any named person, save with leave of the court[16].

Any application with respect to the matters outlined in this chapter will be regarding orders that have previously been made by the court with respect to the child. The Rules require that the court or justices' clerk consider appointing anyone who has acted as guardian ad litem in respect of the child in previous proceedings[17]. Unless there are good reasons for appointing a different guardian ad litem or the original guardian ad litem is no longer available, the guardian ad litem dealing with this matter will be the same one who dealt with the original proceedings.

The applicant will be required to demonstrate that the conditions that brought about the making of the order no longer exist or have been substantially ameliorated such that the order is no longer required. The guardian ad litem must consider the extent of any changes that it is stated have taken place by reference to the original concerns. This may require the guardian ad litem to consider whether any expert evidence is required or indeed whether any expert who was involved in the original proceedings should be required to review the matter during the course of these proceedings.

Where the local authority is making the application, the guardian ad litem should enquire of the local authority whether it proposes to offer the children and/or family any services under Part II of the Children Act 1989. Consideration must be given to whether the discharge of the order would leave the child and/or his family without the necessary support that might ensure successful rehabilitation. Such considerations might well apply with regard to the provision of therapeutic help for children. The abuse suffered by some children might indicate that therapeutic help is required for several years even if rehabilitation to both or one of their parents (or indeed another person) has been successful. The continuing provision of therapeutic help may affect significantly the stability and therefore the success of the rehabilitation programme. The local authority's capacity to provide such therapeutic help or to arrange for its provision by another agency in the absence of any statutory order would need to be carefully scrutinised.

Given the availability to the court of the reports from the previous proceedings, the guardian ad litem's report should consider events that

---

15   CA 1989 s 39(4).
16   CA 1989 s 91(14).
17   FPC (CA 1989) R 1991, r 10(8) and FPR 1991, r 4.10(8).

have taken place since the last proceedings and progress made to date. The matters to be covered in the report would depend upon the nature of the case. It is essential that full consideration is given to the following:

- the wishes and feelings of the child;
- the welfare check-list;
- the applicant's plan and the local authority's care plan (where different);
- contact;
- options available to the court and whether an order is necessary to promote the child's interest and welfare (including the principle of no order).

There will be circumstances where the application is made by one or both parents and is opposed by the local authority. The hearing of the matter will effectively involve a review of all the circumstances, and may require the fullest investigation by the guardian ad litem and a report in the manner of that detailed in chapter four. The guardian ad litem must consider on behalf of the child, in circumstances where she believes the application to be contrary to the child's interests, whether to suggest the court makes an order requiring the parent to obtain leave of the court before he/she can make a future application[18].

Applications may be made by a child of sufficient understanding who would therefore be instructing his own solicitor. The guardian ad litem would have to apply the same principles as outlined above in respect of such an application.

Whether or not the guardian ad litem recommends discharge of the care order or substitution of the care order or the supervision order, she must consider contact and whether the court should make any orders.

---

18   CA 1989 s 91(14).

CHAPTER 21
RESIDENCE ORDER (s 8)

Introduction

"a residence order" means an order settling the arrangements to be made as to the person with whom a child is to live;
(CA 1989 s 8(1))

The making of a residence order with respect to a child who is the subject of a care order discharges the care order.
(CA 1989 s 91(1))

Effect of a residence order

A residence order determines with whom the child is to live and has the following further effects:

- any father granted a residence order who would not otherwise have parental responsibility will also be granted parental responsibility under section 4 regardless of the length of the residence order (section 12(1));
- any person in whose favour a residence order is made acquires parental responsibility for the child while the residence order remains in force (section 12(2));
- those with residence orders who are not parents or guardians may not consent to the child's adoption, or freeing for adoption or appoint a guardian for the child (section 12(3));
- residence orders end when a child reaches the age of 16, unless the court orders otherwise in exceptional circumstances(section 9(6));
- the making of a residence order discharges a care order (section 91(1)).

Without the consent of everyone who has parental responsibility or leave of the court:

- the surname of the child cannot be changed (section 13(1)(a));
- a child may not be removed from the United Kingdom by anyone who has a residence order for more than one month (section 13(1)(b),(2)).

A residence order may not be made, save in exceptional circumstances in respect of a child who has attained the age of sixteen years old (section 9(7)).

Who may apply for a residence order in respect of a child who is the subject of a care order

The category of persons entitled to apply for a residence order or to seek leave to apply for a residence orders is wider than the category of those able to apply for the discharge of a care order. Any person who does not have parental responsibility but has a legitimate interest in the welfare of the child may secure the discharge of the care order by the making of a residence order in their favour.

Those persons entitled to apply for a residence order, or entitled to apply for leave to apply for a residence order, are listed in sections 9 and 10. Section 9(3) covers local authority foster parents and section 10 covers other persons. The list of applicants is as follows:

- any parent or guardian of the child (section 10(4)(a));
- step-parents and former step-parents (section 10(5)(a));
- any person with whom the child has lived for a period of at least three years (or a total of three years within a five year period and the child must have lived with applicant within three months before application) (section 10(5)(b));
- a person who has the consent of the local authority (section 10(5)(c)(ii));
- any other person who has leave of the court (section 10(2)(b)).

Anyone who in the preceding six months was a local authority foster-parent for the child may not apply for leave to apply for a residence order in respect of that child unless[1]:

- he has the consent of the local authority; or
- he is a relative of the child; or
- the child has lived with him for at least three years preceding the application (the three years need not be continuous but must have begun within a period of not more than five years before the application is made[2]).

A child needs the court's leave to apply for a residence order. Leave will be granted if the court is satisfied that he has sufficient understanding to make the application[3].

An application for a residence order in respect of a child who is the subject of a care order, as a means of discharging a care order, is the appropriate course for those persons who do not have parental responsibility, e.g. unmarried fathers, grandparents, other relatives and local authority foster-parents. Those who have parental responsibility and who are thereby entitled to apply for the discharge of a care order would be expected to use that route.

There may be circumstances where it is appropriate for someone who has parental responsibility to obtain the discharge of a care order by applying

---

1   CA 1989 s 9(3).
2   CA 1989 s 9(4).
3   CA 1989 s 10(8) as defined under s 8(2); see chapter 6 – Legal representation.

for a residence order. This is likely where parents are living apart and thereby the court may need to regulate with whom a child should live following the discharge of any care order.

Conditions for making a residence order in respect of a child who is the subject of a care order

As with applications to discharge a care order or vary or discharge a supervision order, the court will need to be satisfied that the child's welfare would be safeguarded by the alteration of the current care arrangements and by changing any orders to which the child is subject.

In proceedings under section 8 the court may consider the full range of orders available to it, and whilst considering any residence application may make a contact order, and attach conditions to any such orders, whether or not any party has made an application for such orders[4].

Guardian ad litem's investigation and report

Matters to be covered by the guardian ad litem in an application for a residence order with respect to a child who is the subject of a care order, are similar to those outlined in the previous chapter when considering the discharge of a care order[5].

An application by an unmarried father, grandparent or other relatives for a residence order may be made with the support of the local authority. Such an application may indeed form part of the local authority's plan. There will, however, be circumstances where the local authority will be opposed to such an application. As outlined in chapter 20, such applications are likely to involve a review of matters since the original order was made.

Applications by a local authority foster parent may or may not have the support of the local authority. The guardian ad litem must consider the local authority care plan, the views of the parents and anyone else who holds parental responsibility, and the wishes and feelings of the child. Where the local authority are opposing the application, the guardian ad litem will need to clarify the local authority's care plan and it implications for the child's placement with the foster parents. It is possible that circumstances may arise where the local authority's plan is for rehabilitation of the child to a particular parent, relative or other person, and that the local authority foster parents are deeply opposed to such a plan. Inevitably, such a situation would involve a full review of matters since the making of the original order, as outlined in chapter 20.

In the event of the court being asked to make a residence order in favour of a local authority foster parent, the guardian ad litem must enquire of the

---

4   CA 1989 s 11(7).
5   See chapter 20 – Discharge of a care or supervision order and variation, substitution or extension of a supervision order and chapter 4 – Guardian ad litem's investigation and report.

local authority whether it will provide the child and applicant any services under Part II of the Children Act 1989 to support the child's continuing placement, and whether the local authority intends continuing to pay any allowances to the applicant.

The guardian ad litem should consider the therapeutic needs of the child and whether the making of a residence order would result in the child having less access to such resources than he might have had whilst the subject of a care order.

Such applications may arise in circumstances where the child has learning difficulties or physical disabilities and the guardian ad litem must consider any implications of the making of such an order for the child and services he may be provided upon obtaining adulthood. The guardian ad litem should also bear in mind that residence orders end when a child reaches 16 years old unless the court orders otherwise in exceptional circumstances. A residence order may not be made with respect to a child who has already obtained the age of 16 years, save in exceptional circumstances[6]. The guardian ad litem must consider particularly in cases of children with learning difficulties or physical disabilities whether such exceptional circumstances exist and the benefit to the child of a residence order extending until the child has obtained the age of 18 years old.

---

6   CA 1989 s 9(7).

CHAPTER 22
CONTACT ORDER (s 34)

Introduction

Butler-Sloss L J observed[1]:

> "The presumption of contact, which has to be for the benefit of the child, has always to be balanced against the long term welfare of the child, particularly where he will live in the future. Contact must not be allowed to de-stablise or endanger the arrangements for the child and in many cases the plans for the child will be decisive of the contact application."

The effect of a contact order on a child who is the subject of a care order

Contact under section 34 has the same meaning as contact under section 8 which states:

> *"a contact order" means an order requiring the person with whom a child lives, or is to live, to allow the child to visit or stay with the person named in the order, or for that person and the child otherwise to have contact with each other;*
>
> *(CA 1989 s 8(1))*

Contact with children who are the subject of care orders is governed by section 34. Before the court makes a care order in respect of a child it must consider the contact arrangements proposed by the local authority and hear the comments of all parties upon those proposals[2].

Local authority's duties with regard to contact for a child in care

> *Where a child is in the care of a local authority, the authority shall (subject to the provisions of this section) allow the child reasonable contact with –*
>
> (a) *his parents;*
> (b) *any guardian of his;*
> (c) *where there was a residence order in force with respect to the child immediately before the care order was made, the person in whose favour the order was made; and*

---

1   Re B (Minors) (Care: Contact: Local Authority's Plans) [1993] 1 FLR 543.
2   CA 1989 s 34(11).

> (d) where, immediately before the care order was made, a person had care of the child by virtue of an order made in the exercise of the High Court's inherent jurisdiction with respect to children, that person.
>
> *(CA 1989 s 34(1))*

The local authority's duties are further clarified in Schedule 2 which states:

> Where a child is being looked after by a local authority, the authority shall, unless it is not reasonably practicable or consistent with his welfare, endeavour to promote contact between the child and –
>
> (a) his parents;
> (b) any person who is not a parent of his but who has parental responsibility for him; and
> (c) any relative, friend or other person connected with him.
>
> *(CA 1989 Sch 2, para 15(1))*

Contact may also be taken to mean keeping a child's parents, and anyone else who may have parental responsibility for him, informed of where the child is being accommodated and of any change of the child's address[3].

Who may apply for a contact order with respect to a child in care

Persons who may apply for a contact order with a child in care are as follows:

- his parents[4];
- any guardian[4];
- any person who had a residence order before the making of a care order[4];
- any person who had care of the child prior to an order being made by the High Court in the exercise of its inherent jurisdiction[4];
- the local authority[5];
- the child[5];
- any person who has obtained the leave of the court[6].

The local authority and the child are the only applicants of those listed above who may apply to the court for an order permitting the local authority to refuse contact between the child and any of those entitled to apply or anyone named in any contact order regarding the child[7]. Applications regarding contact may be lodged by the child as a consequence of the local authority, for whatever reason, not allowing the child to have contact, or sufficient contact, with a particular person (who may also apply).

---

3   CA 1989 Sch 2, para 15(2),(3).
4   CA 1989 s 34(3)(a).
5   CA 1989 s 34(2).
6   CA 1989 s 34(3)(b).
7   CA 1989 s 34(4).

Second and subsequent applications for orders under section 34 are regulated by section 91(17) which states that no one may apply for a contact order within six months after the refusal of their previous application unless the court grants leave. The court may order that a named individual shall not apply for a section 34 order without the leave of the court[8].

Conditions for the making of a contact order with a child in care

On an application for a section 34 contact order, the court is required to decide what level of contact is reasonable for the child by reference to:

- paramountcy of the child's welfare (section 1(1));
- the welfare check-list (section 1(3));
- the no order principle (section 1(5)).

Guardian ad litem's investigation and report

The guardian ad litem must consider the arrangements for contact when the court makes a care order or an interim care order as well as in connection with an application for a section 34 order. The starting point for her investigation is that "the local authority shall . . . allow the child reasonable contact" as outlined in section 34(1). Department of Health guidance[9] regarding contact states:

> "Regular contact with parents, relatives and friends will usually be an important part of the child's upbringing in his new environment and is essential to successful rehabilitation. Lack of contact can, over a period, have vital consequences for the rights of parents and child; it can be a major factor in deciding whether to discharge a care order or to dispense with parental agreement to adoption. This is too important to be regarded as simply a matter of management within the sole control of the local authority . . .
>
> . . . Subject to any court order, it is for the authority to decide what is reasonable contact in the circumstances. The degree of contact should not necessarily remain static; the local authority may plan for the frequency or duration of contact to increase or decrease over time. Again this should be specified in the plan which is prepared and submitted to the court prior to the making of an order. Where possible, the plan should have been discussed with the child and his parents; any disagreements can be resolved by the court making an order as to the degree of contact".

The local authority's plans for the child provide a context for the application, as do the plans of those making the contact application[10]. Where the local

---

8   CA 1989 s 91(14).
9   CA 1989 Guidance and Regulations vol 1: Court Orders, paras 3.77 – 3.78 p 37.
10   See Re B (Minors) (Care: Contact: Local Authority's Plans) [1993] 1 FLR 543 for a detailed analysis of the nature of section 34 contact applications.

authority plans to terminate parental contact and to place a child permanently with an alternative family, a contact application may, if successful, jeopardise the local authority's plans for the child. If the applicant seeks contact for its own sake, the guardian ad litem must evaluate the merits of contact for the child, consider whether it would upset the plans of the local authority, and, if so, whether the child's interests might best be safeguarded by no order for contact.

A contact application may be made with the clear hope that if successful it would alter the local authority's plans to include rehabilitation. The application may be seen as a precursor to an application to discharge a care order. This would inevitably involve a full review of the local authority's plans.

Where the local authority has not been able to carry out its intended plans, perhaps for adoption or long term fostering, a contact application by a parent might also be an attempt to change the local authority's plans so as eventually to lead to rehabilitation. The parent or applicant may be able to demonstrate that their circumstances have changed and that the plans of the local authority have not come to fruition. The guardian ad litem must consider the impact of a change in the contact arrangements (with its consequential effect on the local authority's plan for the child) and whether it would be in the interests of the child for the application to be granted.

After considering all the relevant matters and the local authority's plan and whether there should be a change, the guardian ad litem has to consider whether to recommend that a party should not be able without leave of the court to make a further application for a contact order (section 91(14)), and if so during what period. The guardian ad litem might similarly have to consider whether such a recommendation should be made at the end of care proceedings if contact has been refused after a full hearing and where it is likely that any further application for contact would be detrimental to the child.

CHAPTER 23
CHANGE OF SURNAME
(s 33(7))

Introduction

Applications under section 33(7) to cause a child in care to be known by a new surname, are *specified proceedings* by virtue of the Rules[1]. Before making any application under this section the local authority should have undertaken its prescribed duty to consult everyone who has parental responsibility for the child. A change of surname is a significant matter and will not be allowed merely for convenience[2].

Local authority's duties

Before making any decision with respect to a child whom they are looking after, or proposing to look after, a local authority shall, so far as is reasonably practicable, ascertain the wishes and feelings of –

(a) the child;
(b) his parents;
(c) any person who is not a parent of his, but who has parental responsibility for him; and
(d) any other person whose wishes and feelings the authority consider to be relevant,

regarding the matter to be decided.

(CA 1989 s 22(4))

In making any such decision a local authority shall give due consideration –

(a) having regard to his age and understanding, to such wishes and feelings of the child as they have been able to ascertain;
(b) to such wishes and feelings of any person mentioned in sub-section (4)(b) to (d) as they have been able to ascertain; and
(c) to the child's religious persuasion, racial origin and cultural and linguistic background.

(CA 1989 s 22(5))

---

1   FPC (CA 1989) R 1991, r 2(2)(b) and FPR 1991, r 4.2(2)(b).
2   W v A (Child: Surname) [1981] Fam 14.

Changing the surname of a child in care

While a care order is in force with respect to a child, no person may –

> *(a) cause the child to be known by a new surname; . . .*

without either the written consent of every person who has parental responsibility for the child or the leave of the court.
(CA 1989 s 33(7))

Applications

An application to change a surname of a child in care of the local authority will be made by the local authority. An application will normally be made to the family proceedings court unless there are specified proceedings pending in respect of the child in the county court or High Court, in which case the application should be made to that court.

The child and every person who had parental responsibility prior to the making of a care order in respect of the child will automatically be a respondent to the application. Notice of the proceedings should additionally be served on all the parties to the proceedings where a care order was made.

An application can be made *ex parte*[3] in exceptional circumstances where the child's welfare demands it.

Grounds for giving leave for change of child's surname

Before making an application, the local authority should have sought the permission of everyone who has parental responsibility for the child, and also have ascertained the child's wishes and feelings in this matter. Any application for leave of the court to change the child's surname will therefore arise in circumstances where one or more persons with parental responsibility have refused to agree to the local authority's request.

In considering the application, the court has take into account:

- the paramountcy of the child's welfare (section 1(1));
- the welfare check-list (section 1(3));
- the no order principle (section 1(5));

Guardian ad litem's investigation and report

The guardian ad litem will need to consider the following: –

- the reasons for the request to change the child's surname;

---

3   Re J (A Minor) (Change of Name) [1993] (1FCR 74).

- reasons a party might have for opposing the request;
- the care plan for the child and the impact a change of surname would have on that plan;
- the child's expressed wishes and feelings with respect to a change of surname;
- implications for the child's sense of identity of a change of surname;
- implications for the child's contact with any members of his family;
- implications for the child's future.

There may be several circumstances in which the local authority feels it right to apply to change a child's surname, the most common of which are likely to be:

- child placed securely with long term foster parents, where for whatever reason adoption is not possible;
- child placed with long term foster parents, where there are real concerns that parents or persons who may have abused the child, and who are not allowed contact, might attempt to trace the child;
- child placed with a member of his family, in a situation where an abusive member of his family may not be allowed contact and moreover, the whereabouts of the child and the members of the family with whom he is living should not be divulged to that person.

The guardian ad litem will wish to ensure that the application for leave of the court to change the child's surname is consistent with the care plan. Consideration must be given to:

- the impact on the quality of any contact still taking place with a member of the child's family;
- the likelihood of the child re-establishing contact with his family, and therefore the impact that such a change of surname would have on the possible quality of that contact after the child has attained his majority;
- the impact upon the child's relationship with his wider family, e.g. siblings, cousins, uncles, aunts and grandparents;
- whether members of the child's extended family will alter inheritance plans;
- whether the child's sense of security in a new family unit would be enhanced by a change of surname;
- an evaluation of the nature of any threat to the child's security, and whether a change of surname is actually going to afford the child any more protection.

The impact on the child's sense of identity in all the circumstances outlined above is one of the prime factors to be considered and weighed against other factors. In transracial placements, thought must to be given to the impact that a change of surname might have on both the child's sense of his cultural background, as well as his sense of his racial identity.

CHAPTER 24

REMOVAL OF A CHILD FROM THE COURT'S JURISDICTION (s 33(7) & Sch 2 para 19(1))

Introduction

There are two forms of application which cover a child in care leaving the jurisdiction of the court, either temporarily or permanently. They are as follows:

- Removing a child in care from the United Kingdom (section 33(7));
- Permission for a child in care to live outside England and Wales (Schedule 2, paragraph 19(1)).

These applications are *specified proceedings* by virtue of the Rules[1].

Local authority's duties

The local authority can, under the auspices of a care order, authorise a child to leave the United Kingdom for a period of less than one month. The agreement of everyone who has parental responsibility is not needed.

The local authority's duties with regard to consultations regarding any decision to remove a child from the United Kingdom are set out in section 22[2].

Where the court has given leave for a child to live outside England and Wales, and where the care order has not been revoked, the local authority will have to make arrangements with an equivalent agency in the country in which the child will live so as to ensure that the child receives appropriate support and that the placement is appropriately supervised.

Removing a child in care from the United Kingdom

While a care order is in force with respect to a child, no person may –

(b) remove him from the United Kingdom,

---

1   FPC (CA 1989) R 1991, r 2(2)(c),(d) and FPR 1991, r 4.2(2)(c),(d).
2   CA 1989 s 22(4),(5); see chapter 23 – Change of surname.

without either the written consent of every person who has parental responsibility for the child or the leave of the court.

(CA 1989 s 33(7))

Sub section (7)(b) does not –

    (a) prevent the removal of such a child, for a period of less than one month, by the authority in whose care he is; or

    (b) apply to arrangements for a child to live outside England and Wales (which are governed by paragraph 19 of Schedule 2).

(CA 1989 s 33(8))

Section 33(7)(b)) refers to a child in care being removed from the United Kingdom in circumstances where his removal is only temporary, whether for a holiday or for other purposes. Any decision made by a local authority that it would be in the interests of a child in care to live outside England and Wales would have to be considered under paragraph 19(1) of Schedule 2 referred to later in this chapter.

Applications to remove a child in care from the United Kingdom

Applications to remove a child in the care of the local authority from the United Kingdom will be made by the local authority. Applications will be made to the family proceedings court, unless specified proceedings are pending in respect of the child in the county court or High Court, or orders have been made in respect of the child in the county court or High Court, when the application should be made to that court.

Every person who had parental responsibility prior to the making of a care order in respect of the child and the child will be a respondent to the application.

Grounds for giving leave for a child to be removed from the United Kingdom

Before making any application, the local authority should have sought the permission of everyone who has parental responsibility for the child, and also have ascertained the child's wishes and feelings in this matter. An application, therefore, arises where a person with parental responsibility has refused to agree to the request for the child to be removed from the United Kingdom, or where a child does not agree to such removal. In considering the application, the court has to take into account:

- the paramountcy of the child's welfare (section 1(1));
- the welfare check-list (section 1(3));
- the no order principle (section 1(5)).

Guardian ad litem's investigation and report

Any application will involve at least the removal of the child from the United Kingdom for one month or more. In order to assess the application, the guardian ad litem will need to consider the following:

- the reasons for the application;
- the objections being made by someone with parental responsibility;
- the care plan for the child and the impact any temporary removal from the United Kingdom might have on that plan;
- the child's expressed wishes and feelings with respect to any removal from the United Kingdom;
- implications for any contact arrangements that the child might be having with members of his family or other persons;
- implications for the child's education;
- implications for any therapeutic help or treatment being received by the child;
- the local authority's plans for supervision of the child's placement whilst he is outside the United Kingdom.

The most common circumstances in which an application is made for a child to be removed from the United Kingdom are likely to be:

- a child in care going on holiday outside the United Kingdom for a month or more;
- a local authority seeking to place a child in a residential establishment outside the United Kingdom;
- a child in residential care where the residential unit plan a holiday outside of the United Kingdom that will last for more than one month;
- a child in care travelling abroad with a relative or foster carer in order to further his sense of cultural identity;
- a child placed with prospective adopters who plan to live permanently outside England and Wales, once the adoption order is made, and therefore wish to temporarily reside outside England and Wales for a period of time exceeding one month prior to the hearing of any adoption application.

The child's expressed wishes and feelings regarding the matter have to be ascertained. Where they conflict with either the care plan, the application or the objections of anyone with parental responsibility, the guardian ad litem should offer an opinion promoting the welfare of the child. The effect of any disruption of the contact arrangements upon the child would have to be weighed against the effect of not leaving the United Kingdom with his foster parents or residential unit, and having to be found alternative accommodation.

Approval for a child in care to live outside England and Wales

A local authority may only arrange for, or assist in arranging for, any child in their care to live outside England and Wales with the approval of the court.

(CA 1989 Sch 2, para 19(1))

An order made under paragraph 19(1) of Schedule 2 does not have the effect of discharging a care order.

The local authority may apply to a court under the above paragraph to transfer their responsibilities to the equivalent authorities in Northern Ireland, the Isle of Man or Guernsey[3]. Responsibility for a child who is a subject of an interim care order may not be transferred to any of the above authorities.

Applications for approval for a child in care to live outside England and Wales

Applications for a child in care of the local authority to live outside England and Wales may only be made by the local authority. Applications will normally be made to the family proceedings court, unless there are current specified proceedings pending in respect of the child in the county court or High Court[4]. Applications should normally be transferred to the county court or the High Court.

Every person who had parental responsibility prior to the making of a care order in respect of the child will automatically be a respondent to the application, as will the child. Notice of the proceedings should additionally be served on all parties to the original proceedings where a care order was made.

Grounds for the court giving its approval for a child in care to live outside England and Wales

The court shall not give its approval under sub-paragraph (1) unless it is satisfied that –

    (a) living outside England and Wales would be in the child's best interests;

    (b) suitable arrangements have been, or will be, made for his reception and welfare in the country in which he will live;

    (c) the child has consented to living in that country; and

---

3   CA 1989 s 101; Children (Prescribed Orders – Northern Ireland, Guernsey and the Isle of Man) Regulations 1991, (SI 1991/2032), reg 2.

4   Children (Allocation of Proceedings) Order 1991, (SI 1991/1677), art. 4.

> *(d) every person who has parental responsibility for the child has consented to his living in that country.*
>
> *(CA 1989 Sch 2, para 19(3))*
>
> *Where the court is satisfied that the child does not have sufficient understanding to give or withhold his consent, it may disregard sub-paragraph (3)(c) and give its approval if the child is to live in the country concerned with a parent, guardian, or other suitable persons.*
>
> *(CA 1989 Sch 2, para 19(4))*

A child who has sufficient understanding to give or withhold his consent must give his consent for the court to make any order under this paragraph. The local authority would be expected to have ascertained the child's wishes and feelings regarding the matter prior to making any application.

The consent of a person with parental responsibility can either be given orally in court, or in writing to the justices' clerk or the court and signed by the person giving his consent[5]. The court may disregard the failure to give consent by anyone who has parental responsibility:

> *Where a person whose consent is required by sub-paragraph (3)(d) fails to give his consent, the court may disregard that provision and give its approval if it is satisfied that that person –*
>
> *(a) cannot be found;*
> *(b) is incapable of consenting; or*
> *(c) is withholding his consent unreasonably.*
>
> *(CA 1989 Sch 2, para 19(5))*

The court has to look at the way in which a reasonable person might exercise a responsible choice, taking into account the extent of the sacrifice for the parent concerned[6]. Unlike adoption those who hold parental responsibility do not lose it by virtue of the placement.

The court, in considering the application, has additionally to take into account:

- the paramountcy of the child's welfare (section 1(1));
- the welfare check-list (section 1(3));
- the no order principle (section 1(5)).

Guardian ad litem's investigation and report

The guardian ad litem should ascertain whether the local authority seeks also the discharge of the care order, or whether the local authority feels it should not be discharged, even though the care order will not be enforceable outside England and Wales. If the local authority does not seek the discharge of the care order, the guardian ad litem should ascertain what

---

5   FPC (CA 1989) R 1991, r 25 and FPR 1991, r 4.24.
6   Re G (Minors) (Care: Leave to Place Outside Jurisdiction) [1994] 2 FLR 301.

arrangements the local authority have made with an appropriate agency in the country where the child is going to live for the support and supervision, any financial implications of the child's placement, and how the local authority will exercise its parental responsibility for the child.

The court will look to the guardian ad litem for advice as to whether the proposed arrangements ensure that the child's welfare will be safeguarded and promoted. The Department of Health guidance[7] states:

> "careful consideration needs to be given to the balance to be struck between gaining a settled family life against the loss of familiar people and surroundings".

The Department of Health guidance[8] also suggests that the following information should be provided to the court by the local authority:

- a social history of the child and his family;
- a social history of the proposed carers (if not the family);
- details of the child's periods in care, his placements and any special needs he may have;
- details of planning for the child to live abroad and any preparatory work undertaken with the child to show that he is fully aware of the implications of living in another country;
- report on the home conditions in the place to which the child is to go;
- in circumstances where the child is to join a carer, a report that gives background information about the person's circumstances and suitability;
- arrangements for the child's schooling and the meeting of any special educational needs of the child;
- arrangements to meet specific health needs, including any mental incapacity or physical disability from which the child may suffer;
- confirmation that the local social services agency in the country to which the child would go, are willing to supervise the proposed placement, and any details of their plan, including the management of any placement breakdown and possible return to England and Wales;
- in circumstances where the care order is to remain in force, details from the overseas agency about how a system of supervision will be in place to enable the local authority to carry out its obligations under the relevant placement regulations and the Review of Children's Cases Regulations 1991;
- the child's expressed wishes and feelings with the respect to living outside England and Wales;
- where the child is of sufficient understanding, whether the child consents to the proposed plan or the reasons why he does not consent;
- the views of anyone with parental responsibility on the proposed plan, and whether or not they consent;

---

7   CA 1989 Guidance and Regulations vol 8 – Private Fostering and Miscellaneous, para 4.8 p 38.
8   Ibid para 4.9 p 38.

- if any person with parental responsibility could not be consulted an account of the efforts to consult them;
- the local authority should confirm that the child's passport and any relevant immigration visa requirements are in order;
- where it is planned that the care order would remain in force, details of the local authority's contingency plans to safeguard the child's welfare in the event of the placement breaking down;
- an outline of any proposed travel arrangments, including details of anyone accompanying the child;
- implication for the child's contact with any member of his family;
- where appropriate, plans for sustaining the child's contact with any person with parental responsibility.

Circumstances in which the local authority feels it appropriate to apply for permission for a child to live outside of England Wales may include:

- a child placed securely with long term foster parents who wish to emigrate;
- a child in care who has relatives abroad who are able to look after him, which in this context includes Scotland and Northern Ireland;
- a child in care for whom a long term foster placement or prospective adoptive placement has been identified outside of England and Wales.

Much of the information that the court needs will be provided by the local authority. The guardian ad litem will need to inspect the local authority's records and where there are gaps in the information provided by the local authority, the guardian ad litem will need to conduct interviews in order to provide the court with that information.

Where it is proposed that the child should live outside the jurisdiction of the court, consideration should be given as to whether it is practicable, or in the child's interests, for the child to remain the subject of a care order. The guardian ad litem may wish to consider if any financial assistance is needed and how it could be provided. Whilst a care order is not enforceable outside England and Wales, it may provide a safety net for the child in the event of a placement breakdown whilst outside England and Wales. Equally, consideration might be given, where it is proposed that the child live with its foster parents outside England and Wales, to the making of a residence order in favour of the foster parents (if the foster parents agree), thus revoking the care order and giving the foster parents' parental responsibility for the child[9].

Where the child is of sufficient understanding, and does not consent to live outside England and Wales, the child will instruct his solicitor and the guardian ad litem may need to consider separate representation for herself. The guardian ad litem will need to investigate the child's reasons for not consenting to the proposal and the plans of the local authority.

---

9   The making of a residence order in their favour may result in foster parents losing entitlement to certain local authority allowances.

Clearly, it would be a grave step for the court to agree to a child living outside the court's jurisdiction against that child's wishes. The guardian ad litem might need to discuss with the local authority whether it would be possible for the child to visit the proposed place of residence, so that the child might be able to offer a more informed view about the proposal.

The guardian ad litem should interview all those who hold parental responsibility for the child to ascertain their views about the proposed arrangements. Where anyone holding parental responsibility is opposed to the plan, their reasons should be ascertained. In such circumstances the guardian ad litem will have to advise the court whether she feels consent is being withheld unreasonably[10].

The guardian ad litem should assess whether the chances of rehabilitation of the child with his own family have been properly explored. Any move to live abroad might render rehabilitation impossible.

Where a child who is in care is the subject of a rehabilitation programme with members of his own family, there may be proposals for those members of the family and the child to live outside England and Wales. The guardian ad litem should check whether satisfactory arrangements exist in the proposed country of residence for the continued supervision of the rehabilitation programme, thus ensuring that the child's welfare continues to be safeguarded and promoted.

Appeals

The procedure for appeals against the making of an order authorising the child's removal from the United Kingdom for more than a month is the same as for all applications under Part IV of the Children Act 1989[11]. Where the child's departure is imminent an appellant might wish to apply to the court making the order for a stay of execution of the order pending appeal.

Appeals against a decision for a child to live or not to live outside England and Wales are specifically provided for under Schedule 2[12].

Any party is entitled to appeal against the decision, and has fourteen days in which to lodge an appeal. The court's decision will not have effect during the fourteen days during which an appeal may be made, or whilst an appeal is being determined.

---

10   CA 1989 Sch 2 para 19(5)(c); Re G (Minors) (Care: Leave to Place Outside Jurisdiction) [1994] 2 FLR 301.
11   See chapter 12 – Appeals and judicial review.
12   CA 1989 Sch 2 para 19(7),(8).

CHAPTER 25
SECURE ACCOMMODATION ORDER (s 25)

Introduction

Department of Health guidance[1] states:

> "Restricting the liberty of children is a serious step which must be taken only when there is no appropriate alternative. It must be a 'last resort' in the sense that all else must first have been comprehensively considered and rejected – never because no other placement was available at the relevant time, because of inadequacies in staffing, because the child is simply being a nuisance or runs away from his accommodation and is not likely to suffer significant harm in doing so, and never as a form of punishment. It is important in considering the possibility of a secure placement, that there is a clear view of the aims and objectives of such a placement and that those providing the accommodation can fully meet those aims and objectives. Secure placements once made, should only be for so long as is necessary and unavoidable."

Effect of secure accommodation order

A secure accommodation order is referred to in section 25 as:

> . . . *an order authorising the child to be kept in secure accommodation . . .*
>
> *(CA 1989 s 25(4)*

Secure accommodation is defined as:

> . . . *accommodation provided for the purposes of restricting liberty . . .*
>
> *(CA 1989 s 25(1))*

A secure accommodation order does not require the local authority or other authority to keep a child in secure accommodation for the duration of the authority granted, but rather that they may keep the child in secure accommodation only for so long as they judge that the circumstances warrant the use of such accommodation and the criteria continue to be satisfied.

---

1   CA 1989 Guidance and Regulations vol 1: Court Orders, para 5.1 p 66, and vol 4: Residential Care, para 8.5 p 118.

Duration of secure accommodation orders

The maximum time for which the court can make a secure accommodation order in civil cases on a first application is three months, and upon a second application, up to six months. The time begins to run from the date of the court order and not from the date of placement of the child (if later).

The court may adjourn the proceedings and make an interim secure accommodation order for the period of such adjournment within the above mentioned maximum permitted periods (section 25(5)). The use of an interim secure accommodation order may be to afford time or more time for investigation by the guardian ad litem, who may advise the court as to alternative placements for the child. The best interests of the child will be served if interim orders are kept as short as possible.

Children covered by secure accommodation regulations

Applications for secure accommodation orders are made under section 25 of the Children Act 1989, and the Secure Accommodation Regulations 1991[2].

The regulations do not apply if the child is:

- detained under the Mental Health Act 1983 (except in certain circumstances)[3];
- detained under the Children and Young Persons Act 1933, section 53 (after conviction and sentence for certain grave crimes);

because there is already lawful authority to restrict their liberty.

The following may not have their liberty restricted in any circumstances:

- those over school age and accommodated under section 20(5);
- children kept away from home under a child assessment order (section 43);
- children being kept in police protection[4].

Children who are under thirteen years of age may be placed in secure accommodation, but only where prior approval has been given by the Secretary of State[5].

Appointment of guardian ad litem

Guardians ad litem are only appointed in applications for secure accommodation made in the family proceedings court, county court or High Court. They are not appointed in the youth courts.

---

2 SI 1991/1505.
3 Hereford and Worcester C v S [1993] 1 FCR 653.
4 Children (Secure Accommodation) Regulations 1991, (SI 1991/1505).
5 Ibid reg 4.

Guardians ad litem may not be appointed in the following situations:

- when a child has been remanded in the youth courts under the Children and Young Persons Act 1969, section 23(1)[6];
- when a child has been detained under the Police and Criminal Evidence Act 1984, section 38(6)[7].

When a child has been remanded under section 23(1) of the Children and Young Persons Act 1969 from the crown court an application for secure accommodation should be made in the family proceedings court and a guardian ad litem should be appointed[8].

Who may apply for a secure accommodation order

Secure accommodation may be provided by a range of authorities in a range of establishments, and as such all those authorities may apply for a secure accommodation order. They are as follows:

- a local authority[9];

and in the name of the local authority by:

- a health authority[10];
- a National Health Service Trust[10];
- a local education authority[10];
- a residential care home, nursing home or mental nursing home[11];
- a Youth Treatment Centre Director.

The Secure Accommodation Regulations cover children living in accommodation provided by any of the above authorities and institutions. The only exception is a child being detained under the Mental Health Act 1983, where statutory authority already exists for the restriction of liberty. In practice, nearly all applications will be made by local authorities, private psychiatric hospitals, Health Authorities or NHS Trust Psychiatric Units.

Any of the above mentioned authorities, subject to their being authorised persuant to the Secure Accommodation Regulations regarding provision of secure accommodation, may restrict the liberty of a child without court authority, provided the statutory criteria are met. The maximum permitted period is 72 hours, either consecutively or in aggregate in any period of 28 consecutive days[12]. Where the 72 hour period expires late on a Saturday or Sunday, or during a public holiday, the 72 hour period should be treated as if it did not expire until 12 midday on the first working day after the public holiday or Sunday[13].

---

6   As inserted by the Criminal Justice Act 1991, s 60.
7   Children (Secure Accommodation) Regulations 1991, (SI 1991/1505), reg 6(1).
8   CA 1989 92(2) and Magistrates' Court Act 1980 s 6.
9   Children (Secure Accommodation) Regulations 1991, (SI 1991/1505), reg 8.
10   Children (Secure Accommodation) (No 2) Regulations 1991, (SI 1991/2034), reg 2(1).
11   Ibid, reg 2(2).
12   CA 1989 Guidance and Regulations vol 4: Residential Care, para 8.34 p 124.
13   Ibid, para 8.35 p 124

Applications

Applications must be made to the family proceedings court and will usually be dealt with at that court because of their urgency. Applications may be commenced in the county court or High Court when there are pending proceedings in respect of the same child[14]. Applications can only be transferred to the county court or High Court to be linked with other family proceedings already before such a court in respect of the child which arise out of the same circumstances as gave rise to the proceedings to be transferred[15].

The applicant should serve the application and notice of the proceedings at least one day before the directions appointment or hearing upon the following who are automatically respondents[16]:

- the child;
- everyone with parental responsibility;
- if the child is the subject of a care order, those persons who had parental responsibility immediately prior to the making of that order.

Notice must be given to:

- any local authority which is providing accommodation for the child;
- the child's parents;
- if the child is in a refuge[17], the person providing the refuge.

If the child is already in secure accommodation notice must also be given to:

- the child's independent visitor;
- any other persons the local authority considers should be informed[18].

Criteria for the restriction of liberty

Subject to the following provisions of this section, a child who is being looked after by a local authority may not be placed, and, if placed, may not be kept, in accommodation provided for the purpose of restricting liberty ("secure accommodation") unless it appears –

(a) that –

(i) he has a history of absconding and is likely to abscond from any other description of accommodation; and

(ii) if he absconds, he is likely to suffer significant harm; or

---

14   Children (Allocation of Proceedings) Order 1991, (SI 1991/1677), art 3(3).
15   Children (Allocation of Proceedings) Order 1991, (SI 1991/1677), art 7(3).
16   FPC (CA 1989) R 1991, Sch 2 Column (iii) and FPR 1991, Appendix 3 Column (iii).
17   Refuge certified under CA 1989 s 51(1),(2).
18   Children (Secure Accommodation) Regulations 1991, (SI 1991/1505), reg 14.

> (b) that if he is kept in any other description of accommodation he is likely to injure himself or other persons.
>
> *(CA 1989 s 25(1))*

Harm in the context of section 25(1) has the same meaning as in applications for care or supervision orders and thereby includes ill-treatment or the impairment of health or development, development meaning physical, intellectual, emotional, social or behavioural development (section 31(9)). Whether the harm that the child is likely to suffer is significant or not is determined by reference to section 31(10), which states that the child's health or development should be compared with that which would reasonably be expected of a similar child.

In secure accommodation proceedings under the Children Act 1989, the welfare of the child is not the court's paramount consideration[19]. An application for a secure accommodation order is not made under Part IV of the Children Act 1989, accordingly the welfare check-list in section 1(3) is "not of particular relevance although not irrelevant"[20]. The wishes and feelings of the child will be considered by the court when considering the application even though there is no statutory requirement to do so[20].

The court cannot make a secure accommodation order or an interim secure accommodation order unless the child is legally represented or has been offered legal representation and refused to accept it.

The court has the duty to ensure the promotion of the child's welfare and thereby ensure that the child is not unnecessarily or inappropriately subject to secure accommodation. Department of Health guidance[21] referring to the no order principle[22] states:

> "The court must therefore also be satisfied that the order will positively contribute to the child's welfare and must not make an order unless it considers that doing so would be better for the child than making no order at all."

However, under section 22(6):

> If it appears to a local authority that it is necessary, for the purpose of protecting members of the public from serious injury, to exercise their powers with respect to a child whom they are looking after in a manner which may not be consistent with their duties under this section, they may do so.
>
> *(CA 1989 s 22(6))*

Guardian ad litem's investigation and report

Secure accommodation applications may arise in a variety of circumstances. A guardian ad litem may have less than 24 hours' notice of

---

19   M v Birmingham City Council [1994] 2 FLR 141; Re M (Secure Accommodation Order) [1995] 1 FLR.

20   Hereford and Worcester County Council v S [1993] 2 FLR 360.

21   CA 1989 Guidance and Regulations, vol 1: Court Orders, para 5.7 p 67.

22   CA 1989 s 1(5).

her appointment to a case by the time that notice has been lodged with the court and the court has been able to make the appointment. Conversely the guardian ad litem may already have been involved in the case if there were previous or current applications before the court, and thereby have some background knowledge about the circumstances.

The guardian ad litem must ensure that the child is legally represented. The guardian ad litem should ascertain if a solicitor has previously acted or is currently acting for the child. A solicitor already appointed for the child or who has acted before for the child may not be on the Children Panel and may have had little experience of public law cases under the Children Act 1989.

Where the guardian ad litem is concerned that the child may not be capable of giving sufficient instructions or extremely limited instructions, the guardian ad litem should discuss the matter with the child's solicitor. The solicitor is also under a duty to consider whether the child is able to give independent instructions.

It is likely that unless the child is suffering psychiatric illness, is severely emotionally and behaviourally disturbed or simply refuses to talk to a solicitor, that the child may be capable of giving sufficient instruction to a solicitor[23]. The guardian ad litem may have to decide with the child's solicitor in a relatively short space of time whether the guardian ad litem should apply to be separately represented, if the child is giving instructions that conflict with those of the guardian ad litem. The guardian ad litem is under a duty to advise the court of any conflict between her instructions and those of the child[24]. The guardian ad litem would not be eligible for legal aid and must apply to the panel manager to fund the cost of that separate representation.

Where the child's solicitor, after taking appropriate professional advice believes the child is no longer capable of giving independent instructions, an order may direct that the guardian ad litem instructs the child's solicitor. This step needs careful consideration because in circumstances where the guardian ad litem agrees with the local authority's application, it may effectively leave the possible articulation of any opposition to the application to the parents. Furthermore, it is possible that the parents might themselves in such circumstances agree with the local authority and guardian ad litem and thereby the court would not be able to hear any arguments against the making of an order. The guardian ad litem has a clear responsibility to articulate the wishes and feelings of the child and, where possible, any opinions the child holds as to whether he should be in secure accommodation.

The guardian ad litem will wish to consider the following in respect of the criteria[25]:

---

23   See chapter 3 – Power and duties of the guardian ad litem, and chapter 6 – Legal representation.
24   FPC (CA 1989) R 1991 r 11(3) and FPR 1991 r 4.11(3); see chapter 3 – Powers and duties of the guardian ad litem.
25   CA 1989 s 25(1).

- any harm that the child might suffer or cause to others if kept in any other form of accommodation;
- whether the local authority's decision to use secure accommodation has been taken at an appropriate level of seniority in the local authority;
- whether secure accommodation is the only appropriate method for dealing with the child;
- whether alternatives for the child have been considered and rejected;
- whether the local authority has a clear view of the aims and objectives of such a placement;
- whether there is either a care plan or a provisional care plan;
- the proposed duration of the order, and whether a shorter term would be sufficient.

Consideration will need to be given to the evidence that the local authority is bringing to support their case. The guardian ad litem will need to be mindful that any order should be made for the child's protection and not as a form of punishment (save for the purpose of protecting members of the public from serious injury in respect of a child looked after[26]). It is possible that children who have suffered serious and grave abuse themselves will (because of the level of disturbance that is induced) be the subject of such applications, and care will need to be exercised by the placing authority to ensure that they are not subject to further abuse by being placed in a secure unit.

When considering a child's history of absconding, the following factors should be taken into account:

- whether the child injured himself or others;
- any harm that the child suffered whilst absconding;
- where the child ran to;
- the child's associates;
- over what period has the absconding taken place and with what frequency;
- did the child commit any offences;
- did the child remain near the establishment or home;
- did the child return voluntarily;
- what were the reasons for running away;
- do other residents at the establishment run away and with what frequency, and why;
- is the child's behaviour a reflection of a pattern of the institution?

The child's views and feelings should be explored and presented to the court. This will include a consideration of:

- whether the child understands the purpose of the hearing;
- whether his capabilities or understanding are permanently or temporarily impaired, whether by medication, learning difficulty or psychiatric illness;

---

26   CA 1989 s 22(6).

- whether the child has been persuaded to agree to secure accommodation;
- whether the child has views as to any form of alternative accommodation that might meet his needs.

The characteristics of the secure placement that is proposed for the child should be considered and investigated with the particular needs of the child in mind and in the context of the care plan proposed by the local authority. This should include consideration of:

- the age, sex and race of other residents;
- the number of section 53 (punishment for certain grave crimes) detainees[27];
- the number of children on remand;
- the number of Police and Criminal Evidence Act 1984 detainees;
- whether, in the case of a psychiatric hospital, there is sufficient evidence that the child suffers from a psychiatric illness.

Additionally, in respect of section 25(1)(b), the guardian ad litem will require information about the child's physical and mental health. She will need to know if the child has previously tried to harm himself and she will scrutinise carefully the applicant's reasons for saying that the child is likely to injure himself or other persons. The child may be suicidal or may have suffered abuse themselves and have commenced abusing other children and be a danger to them. If the local authority do not produce any expert medical evidence from a child psychiatrist the guardian ad litem will want to consider whether she should seek to obtain any such evidence, although this may not be possible in the short time available for her to complete her enquiries.

Given that placement in secure accommodation should be a "last resort", the guardian ad litem should investigate to what extent other forms of accommodation have been tried, whether other alternative forms of accommodation exist and whether those possibilities have been pursued and exhausted by those making the application.

The reasoning for the local authority's application should be inspected carefully. The child may have particular treatment needs which, for whatever reason, appear to be only provided in secure accommodation. This is not a reason for restricting a child's liberty but arrangements should be considered for the treatment to be provided at another form of accommodation that can contain the child.

If the guardian ad litem is of a view that a secure accommodation order is required, she should seek to recommend the minimum time necessary that is possible[28], given the needs of the child and the need to protect others from serious injury.

---

27   Children and Young Persons Act 1933.
28   W v North Yorkshire CC [1993] 1 FCR 693.

Appeals

Appeals against the making of a secure accommodation order by a family proceedings court are made to the High Court. Appeals from a district judge sitting in the country court are made to a circuit judge in the county court or the High Court. Appeals from a circuit judge in the county court or from the High Court are made to the Court of Appeal. When the appeal is against the making of an order, the child may be kept in secure accommodation until that appeal is heard. When the appeal is against the refusal of a court to make such an order, the child may not be detained in secure accommodation during the consideration of the appeal[29].

---

29   CA 1989 Guidance and Regulations vol 4: Residential Care, para 8.49 p 127.

APPENDIX I

THE OFFICIAL SOLICITOR

BEST PRACTICE

on his appointment as guardian ad litem in family proceedings

References:

- Lord Chancellor's Direction of 7/10/91 (reported at [1991] 2 FLR 471)
- Court Business, January 1993 BS480 (reported in Family Law, February 1993)

The Official Solicitor and the Children Act Advisory Committee have issued this note in the hope that it will assist the courts and the profession in securing the services of the Official Solicitor in cases in which his appointment is considered appropriate, and in avoiding delay in undertaking his investigations.

Appointment as guardian ad litem of the child who is the subject of the proceedings

In specified ("public law") proceedings under the Children Act 1989, the Official Solicitor may only be appointed to act as the child's guardian ad litem in the High Court.

In private law proceedings under the 1989 Act he may act as the child's guardian ad litem in the High Court and county court but not the family proceedings court.

The criteria for the appointment of the Official Solicitor as the guardian ad litem of the subject child include cases in which there is disputed medical evidence or medical opinion is at variance, where there is a substantial foreign element, where there are special or exceptional points of law, or where he is already acting for the child in other proceedings.

Subject to Rule 9.2A of the Family Proceedings Rules 1991, the Official Solicitor may also act as the next friend of a child seeking leave to make an application under the 1989 Act or making an application in other family proceedings.

The Official Solicitor can also be appointed to act as the child's guardian ad litem in adoption and freeing proceedings in the High Court (Adoption Rules 1989 r 6(4) and 18(4)) and as the guardian ad litem of a child who is the subject of wardship proceedings or proceedings under the inherent jurisdiction of the High Court.

Appointment as guardian ad litem of an adult party who is under mental disability or minor party other than the child who is the subject of the proceedings

In the absence of any other suitable or willing persons, the Official Solicitor is available to be appointed in the High Court (pursuant to RSC 0.82 r 2) or the county court (pursuant to CCR 1981 Ord 10. r 1) as the guardian ad litem (or next friend) of:

- an adult party who is suffering from mental disorder within the meaning of the Mental Health Act 1983 to an extent that renders him/her incapable of managing his or her property and affairs (medical evidence confirming this must be obtained by the Official Solicitor before he can accept the appointment); or
- (subject to FPR 1991 r 9.2A) a minor party other than the child who is the subject of the proceedings

Orders appointing the Official Solicitor should be expressed as being made subject to his consent. To ensure that he is allowed sufficient time to undertake the investigation he considers necessary in any particular matters, a substantive hearing date should not be fixed without prior consultation between the court listing officer and the Official Solicitor's caseworker.

APPENDIX II
REFERENCES

The Children Act 1989 Guidance and Regulations, volumes 1–10, HMSO, 1991.

The Children Act Advisory Committee: Annual Report 1991/92, The Lord Chancellor's Department.

The Children Act Advisory Committee: Annual Report 1992/93, The Lord Chancellor's Department.

The Children Act Advisory Committee: Annual Report 1993/94, The Lord Chancellor's Department.

Children Act Manual, Masson and Morris, Sweet and Maxwell, 1992.

Children in Public Care, HMSO, 1991.

Children Law and Practice, Hershman and McFarlane, Family Law, 1994.

Clarke Hall & Morrison on Children, Butterworths, 1994.

Guide to Good Practice for Solicitors Acting for Children, Solicitors Family Law Association, 1994.

Manual of Practice Guidance for Guardians ad Litem and Reporting Officers, HMSO, 1992.

Protecting Children: A Guide to Social Workers undertaking a Comprehensive Assessment, HMSO, 1988.

Memorandum of Good Practice, HMSO, 1990.

APPENDIX III
MEMBERS OF THE REFERENCE GROUP

Mrs Margaret Adcock

Social Work Consultant and Guardian ad litem

Mr Jim Baker

Deputy Official Solicitor, Official Solicitor's Office

Dr Arnon Bentovim

Child and Family Psychiatrist, Great Ormond Street Hospital for Children NHS Trust and the Tavistock Clinic

District Judge Caddick

Care Centre District Judge, Medway County Court

The Hon Mr Justice Cazalet

High Court Judge (Family Division)

Mr David Cook

Solicitor in Private Practice, Daniel and Edwards, Ramsgate, Member of the Children Panel

Mrs Edwina Greenwell

Panel Manager for the Bradford, Leeds, Calderdale Panel of Guardians ad Litem and Reporting Officers

Ms Sue Hardy

Guardian ad litem, and Training Officer for the National Association of Guardians ad Litem and Reporting Officers

His Honour Judge Hedley

Nominated Care Judge, Liverpool Combined Courts Centre

Mr Geoffrey Horner

Team Manager, London Borough of Croydon Social Services Department

Mr Ron Jeffries

Deputy Chairman, Redbridge Magistrates, and Deputy Chairman, Family Proceedings Court, Redbridge

Ms Jo Mason

Social Worker, Great Ormond Street Hospital for Children NHS Trust

Mr Mike Oldham	Guardian ad litem
Mr Bernard O'Sullivan	Barrister, 2 Harcourt Buildings, Temple
Mrs Joy Owen	Panel Manager, Kent Panel of Guardians ad Litem and Reporting Officers
Ms Peggy Ray	Solicitor in Private Practice, Goodman Ray, London, Member of Children Panel
Mrs Pauline Robertson	Senior Solicitor, London Borough of Bromley
His Honour Judge Sessions	Nominated Care Judge, Medway County Court
Ms Kath Tunstall	Area Manager, Leeds City Council Social Services Department
Ms Claire Turnbull	Deputy Chief Clerk to the Justices, Inner London SW Magistrates Court
Mr Roger Vobe	Guardian ad litem
Mr Tony Wells	Director of Development, Council for Family Proceedings, University of Bristol

INDEX

Page numbers given in *italic* indicate tables.

Printed in the United Kingdom for TSO
N126620 C5 1/03 9385 18655